OUT OF MY MIND

OUT OF MY MIND

SHARON M. DRAPER

THORNDIKE PRESS
A part of Gale, a Cengage Company

Farmington Hills, Mich • San Francisco • New York • Waterville, Maine
Meriden, Conn • Mason, Ohio • Chicago

Recommended for Middle Readers.
Copyright © 2010 by Sharon M. Draper.
"Elvira" copyright © 1965 Sony/ATV Music Publishing LLC. All rights administered by Sony/ATV Music Publishing LLC. 8 Music Square West, Nashville, Tn 37203. All rights reserved. Used by permission.
Thorndike Press, a part of Gale, a Cengage Company.

Thorndike Press® Large Print Mini-Collections.
The text of this Large Print edition is unabridged.
Other aspects of the book may vary from the original edition.
Set in 16 pt. Plantin.

LIBRARY OF CONGRESS CIP DATA ON FILE.
CATALOGUING IN PUBLICATION FOR THIS BOOK
IS AVAILABLE FROM THE LIBRARY OF CONGRESS

ISBN-13: 978-1-4328-6075-2 (hardcover)

Published in 2018 by arrangement with Atheneum Books for Young Readers, an imprint of Simon & Schuster Children's Publishing Division

Printed in Mexico
3 4 5 6 7 8 23 22 21 20 19

ACKNOWLEDGMENTS

With deep appreciation, I'd like to thank all the wonderful individuals who dedicate their lives to children with special needs.

I'd like to offer my special thanks and gratitude to the patient and devoted caregivers at Echoing Lake Facilities, The Renouard Home, The Lucy Idol Center, Camp Cheerful, Stepping Stones, Camp Allyn, Bobbie Fairfax School, and Roselawn Condon School (extra thanks to Daphne Robinson).

Thank you to my friend Karen Brantley, who really understands it all!

And special thanks to my editor Caitlyn Dlouhy for her amazing skill, vision, and that green editing pen!

To my daughter,
Wendy Michelle Draper,
with love

CHAPTER 1

Words.

I'm surrounded by thousands of words. Maybe millions.

Cathedral. Mayonnaise. Pomegranate.
Mississippi. Neapolitan. Hippopotamus.
Silky. Terrifying. Iridescent.
Tickle. Sneeze. Wish. Worry.

Words have always swirled around me like snowflakes — each one delicate and different, each one melting untouched in my hands.

Deep within me, words pile up in huge drifts. Mountains of phrases and sentences and connected ideas. Clever expressions. Jokes. Love songs.

From the time I was really little — maybe just a few months old — words were like sweet, liquid gifts, and I drank them like lemonade. I could almost taste them. They made my jumbled thoughts and feelings have substance. My parents have always blanketed me with conversation. They chattered and babbled. They verbalized and vocalized. My father sang to me. My mother whispered her strength into my ear.

Every word my parents spoke to me or about me I absorbed and kept and remembered. All of them.

I have no idea how I untangled the complicated process of words and thought, but it happened quickly and naturally. By the time I was two, all my memories had words, and all my words had meanings.

But only in my head.

I have never spoken one single word. I am almost eleven years old.

CHAPTER 2

I can't talk. I can't walk. I can't feed myself or take myself to the bathroom. Big bummer.

My arms and hands are pretty stiff, but I can mash the buttons on the TV remote and move my wheelchair with the help of knobs that I can grab on the wheels. I can't hold a spoon or a pencil without dropping it. And my balance is like zip — Humpty Dumpty had more control than I do.

When people look at me, I guess they see a girl with short, dark, curly hair strapped into a pink wheelchair. By the way, there is nothing cute about a pink wheelchair. Pink doesn't change a thing.

They'd see a girl with dark brown eyes that are full of curiosity. But one of them is slightly out of whack.

Her head wobbles a little.

Sometimes she drools.

She's really tiny for a girl who is age ten

and three quarters.

Her legs are very thin, probably because they've never been used.

Her body tends to move on its own agenda, with feet sometimes kicking out unexpectedly and arms occasionally flailing, connecting with whatever is close by — a stack of CDs, a bowl of soup, a vase of roses.

Not a whole lot of control there.

After folks got finished making a list of my problems, they might take time to notice that I have a fairly nice smile and deep dimples — I think my dimples are cool.

I wear tiny gold earrings.

Sometimes people never even ask my name, like it's not important or something. It is. My name is Melody.

I can remember way back to when I was really, really young. Of course, it's hard to separate real memories from the videos of me that Dad took on his camcorder. I've watched those things a million times.

Mom bringing me home from the hospital — her face showing smiles, but her eyes squinted with worry.

Melody tucked into a tiny baby bathtub. My arms and legs looked so skinny. I didn't splash or kick.

Melody propped with blankets on the living room sofa — a look of contentment on my face. I never cried much when I was a baby; Mom swears it's true.

Mom massaging me with lotion after a bath — I can still smell the lavender — then wrapping me in a fluffy towel with a little hood built into one corner.

Dad took videos of me getting fed, getting changed, and even me sleeping. As I got older, I guess he was waiting for me to turn over, and sit up, and walk. I never did.

But I did absorb everything. I began to recognize noises and smells and tastes. The *whump* and *whoosh* of the furnace coming alive each morning. The tangy odor of heated dust as the house warmed up. The feel of a sneeze in the back of my throat.

And music. Songs floated through me and stayed. Lullabies, mixed with the soft smells of bedtime, slept with me. Harmonies made me smile. It's like I've always had a painted musical sound track playing background to my life. I can almost hear colors and smell images when music is played.

Mom loves classical. Big, booming Beethoven symphonies blast from her CD player all day long. Those pieces always seem to be bright blue as I listen, and they smell like fresh paint.

Dad is partial to jazz, and every chance he gets, he winks at me, takes out Mom's

13

Mozart disc, then pops in a CD of Miles Davis or Woody Herman. Jazz to me sounds brown and tan, and it smells like wet dirt. Jazz music drives Mom crazy, which is probably why Dad puts it on.

"Jazz makes me itch," she says with a frown as Dad's music explodes into the kitchen.

Dad goes to her, gently scratches her arms and back, then engulfs her in a hug. She stops frowning. But she changes it back to classical again as soon as Dad leaves the room.

For some reason, I've always loved country music — loud, guitar-strumming, broken-heart music. Country is lemons — not sour, but sugar sweet and tangy. Lemon cake icing, cool, fresh lemonade! Lemon, lemon, lemon! Love it.

When I was really little, I remember sitting in our kitchen, being fed breakfast by Mom, and a song came on the radio that made me screech with joy.

So I'm singin'
Elvira, Elvira
My heart's on fire, Elvira
Giddy up oom poppa oom poppa mow mow
Giddy up oom poppa oom poppa mow mow
Heigh-ho Silver, away

How did I already know the words and the rhythms to that song? I have no idea. It must have seeped into my memory somehow — maybe from a radio or TV program. Anyway, I almost fell out of my chair. I scrunched up my face and jerked and twitched as I tried to point to the radio. I wanted to hear the song again. But Mom just looked at me like I was nuts.

How could she understand that I loved the song "Elvira" by the Oak Ridge Boys when I barely understood it myself? I had no way to explain how I could smell freshly sliced lemons and see citrus-toned musical notes in my mind as it played.

If I had a paintbrush . . . wow! What a painting that would be!

But Mom just shook her head and kept on spooning applesauce into my mouth. There's so much my mother doesn't know.

I suppose it's a good thing to be unable to forget anything — being able to keep every instant of my life crammed inside my head. But it's also very frustrating. I can't share any of it, and none of it ever goes away.

I remember stupid stuff, like the feel of a lump of oatmeal stuck on the roof of my mouth or the taste of toothpaste not rinsed off my teeth.

The smell of early-morning coffee is a

permanent memory, mixed up with the smell of bacon and the background yakking of the morning news people.

Mostly, though, I remember words. Very early I figured out there were millions of words in the world. Everyone around me was able to bring them out with no effort.

The salespeople on television: *Buy one and get two free! For a limited time only.*

The mailman who came to the door: *Mornin', Mrs. Brooks. How's the baby?*

The choir at church: *Hallelujah, hallelujah, amen.*

The checkout clerk at the grocery store: *Thanks for shopping with us today.*

Everybody uses words to express themselves. Except me. And I bet most people don't realize the real power of words. But I do.

Thoughts need words. Words need a voice.

I love the smell of my mother's hair after she washes it.

I love the feel of the scratchy stubble on my father's face before he shaves.

But I've never been able to tell them.

CHAPTER 3

I guess I figured out I was different a little at a time. Since I never had trouble thinking or remembering, it actually sort of surprised me that I couldn't do stuff. And it made me angry.

My father brought home a small stuffed cat for me when I was really little — less than a year old, I'm sure. It was white and soft and just the right size for chubby baby fingers to pick up. I was sitting in one of those baby carriers on the floor — strapped in and safe as I checked out my world of green shag carpet and matching sofa. Mom placed the toy cat in my hands, and I smiled.

"Here, Melody. Daddy brought you a play-pretty," she cooed in that high-pitched voice that adults use with children.

Now, what's a "play-pretty"? As if it's not hard enough figuring out real stuff, I have to figure out the meanings of made-up words!

But I loved the soft coolness of the little cat's fur. Then it fell on the floor. Dad placed it in my hands the second time. I really wanted to hold it and hug it. But it fell on the floor once more. I remember I got mad and started to cry.

"Try again, sweetie," Dad said, sadness decorating the edges of his words. "You can do it." My parents placed the cat in my hands again and again. But every single time my little fingers could not hold it, and it tumbled back down to the carpet.

I did my own share of tumbling onto that rug. I guess that's why I remember it so well. It was green and ugly when you looked at it up close. I think shag carpeting was outdated even before I was born. I had lots of chances to figure out how the threads of a rug are woven as I lay there waiting for someone to pick me up. I couldn't roll over, so it was just an irritated me, the shag rug, and the smell of spilled sour soy milk in my face until I got rescued.

My parents would prop me up on the floor with pillows on either side of me when I wasn't in the baby seat. But I'd see a sunbeam coming through the window, turn my head to watch the little dust things that floated in it, and *bam,* I'd be face-first on the floor. I'd shriek, one of them would pick me up, quiet me, and try to balance me better within the cushions. Still I'd fall again in a few minutes.

But then Dad would do something funny, like try to jump like the frog we were watching on *Sesame Street,* and it would make me giggle. And I'd fall over again. I didn't *want* to fall or even mean to. I couldn't help it. I had no balance at all. None.

I didn't understand at the time, but my father did. He would sigh and pull me up onto his lap. He'd hug me close and hold up the little cat, or whatever toy I seemed to be interested in, so I could touch it.

Even though he sometimes made up his own vocabulary, Dad never spoke baby talk to me like my mother did. He always spoke to me as if he were talking to a grown-up, using real words and assuming I would understand him. He was right.

"Your life is not going to be easy, little Melody," he'd say quietly. "If I could switch places with you, I'd do it in a heartbeat. You know that, don't you?"

I just blinked, but I got what he meant. Sometimes his face would be wet with tears. He'd take me outside at night and whisper in my ear about the stars and the moon and the night wind.

"The stars up there are putting on a show

19

just for you, kid," he'd say. "Look at that amazing display of sparkle! And feel that wind? It's trying to tickle your toes."

And during the day he would sometimes take off all the blankets that my mother insisted I be wrapped in and let me feel the warmth of the sun on my face and legs.

He had placed a bird feeder on our porch, and we would sit there together as the birds darted in, picking up seeds one at a time.

"That red one is a cardinal," he'd tell me, and "that one over there is a blue jay. They don't like each other much." And he'd chuckle.

What Dad did most was to sing to me. He has a clear voice that seems made for songs like "Yesterday" and "I Want to Hold Your Hand." Dad loves the Beatles. No, there's no figuring out parents and why they like stuff.

I've always had very good hearing. I remember listening to the sound of my father's car as he drove up our street, pulled into the driveway, and rustled in his pocket to find his house keys. He'd toss them on the bottom step, then I'd hear the sound of the refrigerator door open — twice. The first time he'd get something cold to drink. The second time he'd search for a huge hunk of Muenster cheese. Dad loves cheese. It doesn't agree with his digestive system very well, though. Dad also has the loudest, stinkiest farts in creation. I don't know how he manages to control them at work, or even if he does, but when he'd get home, he'd let them loose. They'd start as he walked up the stairs.

Step, fart.
Step, fart.
Step, fart.

I'd be laughing by the time he got to my room, and he'd lean over my bed and kiss me. His breath always smelled like peppermints.

When he could, Dad read to me. Even though I know he had to be tired, he'd smile, pick out a book or two, and I'd get to go to *Where the Wild Things Are,* or to where *The Cat in the Hat* was making a mess.

I probably knew the words by heart before he did. *Goodnight, Moon. Make Way for Ducklings.* Dozens more. The words to every single book my father ever read to me are forever tucked inside.

Here's the thing: I'm ridiculously smart, and I'm pretty sure I have a photographic memory. It's like I have a camera in my head, and if I see or hear something, I click it, and it stays.

I saw a special on PBS once on children

who were geniuses. These kids could remember complicated strands of numbers and recall words and pictures in correct sequence and quote long passages of poetry. So can I.

I remember the toll-free number from every infomercial, and the mailing addresses and websites, too. If I ever need a new set of knives or the perfect exercise machine, I've got that information on file.

I know the names of the actors and actresses of all the shows, what time each program comes on, which channel, and which shows are repeats. I even remember the dialogue from each show and the commercials in between.

Sometimes I wish I had a delete button in my head.

I have a television remote control clicker attached to my wheelchair, very close to my right hand. On the left side I have a remote for the radio. I have enough control in my fist and thumbs to push the buttons so I can change the station, and I'm *really* glad of that! Twenty-four hours of big-time wrestling or the home shopping station can drive a person nuts! I can adjust the volume and even play DVDs if someone has popped one in the player for me. Lots of times I watch Dad's old videos of me.

But I also like the cable channels that talk about stuff like kings and the kingdoms they conquered or doctors and the diseases they cured. I've seen specials on volcanoes, shark attacks, dogs born with two heads, and the mummies of Egypt. I remember them all. Word for word.

Not that it does me a lot of good. Nobody knows it's there but me. Not even my mother, although she has this "Mom sense" that knows I understand stuff. But even that has its limits.

Nobody gets it. Nobody. Drives me crazy.

So every once in a while I *really* lose control. I mean really. My arms and legs get all tight and lash out like tree limbs in a storm. Even my face draws up. I sometimes can't breathe real well when this happens, but I have to because I need to screech and scream and jerk. They're not seizures. Those are medical and make you go to sleep.

These things — I call them my "tornado explosions" — are pieces of me. All the stuff that does not work gets balled up and hyped up. I can't stop, even though I want to, even though I know I'm freaking people out. I lose myself. It can get kinda ugly.

Once, when I was about four, Mom and I were in one of those superstores that sells everything from milk to sofas. I was still small enough to fit in the child seat in the front of the cart. Mom always came prepared and stuffed pillows on each side of me so I wouldn't tilt. Everything was fine. She tossed toilet paper and mouthwash and detergent into the cart, and I looked around, enjoying the ride.

Then, in the toy section, I saw them. Brightly colored packages of plastic blocks. Just that morning I had seen a warning on television about that toy — they were being recalled because the blocks had been painted with lead paint. Several children had already been hospitalized with lead poisoning, the report had said. But there they were — still on the shelf.

I pointed to them.

Mom said, "No, sweetie. You don't need those. You have enough toys."

I pointed again and screeched. I kicked my feet.

"No!" Mom said more forcefully. "You are not going to have a tantrum on me!"

I didn't want the blocks. I wanted to tell her they were dangerous. I wanted her to tell somebody to get rid of them before a child got sick. But all I could do was scream and point and kick. So I did. I got louder.

Mom rushed out of the toy section, pushing the cart real fast. "Stop it!" she cried out at me.

I couldn't. It made me so angry that I couldn't tell her. The tornado took over. My arms became fighting sticks, my legs became weapons. I kicked at her with my feet. I screamed. I kept pointing in the direction of those blocks.

People stared. Some pointed. Others looked away.

Mom got to the door of the store, yanked me out of the cart, and left it with all her selections sitting there. She was almost in tears when she got to the car. As she buckled me in my seat, she almost screamed at me, "What is *wrong* with you?"

Well, she knew the answer to that one, but she knew that was not my usual behavior. I gulped, sniffed, and finally calmed down. I hoped the people at the store watched the news.

When we got home, she called the doctor and told him about my crazy behavior. He sent a prescription for a sedative, but Mom didn't give it to me. The crisis was over by then.

I don't think Mom ever figured out what I was trying to say that day.

CHAPTER 4

Doctors. Where do I start? Doctors *really* don't get me. Mom's a nurse, so I guess she speaks their language, but they sure don't know how to talk to me.

I've seen dozens of doctors in my life, who all try to analyze me and figure me out. None of them can fix me, so I usually ignore them and act like the retarded person they think I am. I paste on a blank look, focus on one wall, and pretend their questions are too hard for me to understand. It's sort of what they expect anyway.

When I turned five, it was time to think about enrolling me in school. So my mother took me to a doctor whose job it was to figure out how smart I was. She wheeled me in, locked the brake so my wheelchair would not roll, and made sure the lap strap was fastened. When my seat belt comes undone — and it does every once in a while — I slide out of that wheelchair like a piece

26

of wet spaghetti.

The specialist was a very large man. The bottom button of his shirt had come undone, and his stomach poked through above his belt. Gross!

"My name is Dr. Hugely," he said in a booming voice.

For real. I couldn't make this stuff up.

"We're going to play a game today, okay? I'll ask you some questions, and you get to play with the toys here. Won't that be fun?"

I knew it would be a long, long hour.

He brought out a stack of well-used, hopefully not lead-tainted, wood blocks, then leaned in so close to me, I could see the pores in his face. Gross! "Can you stack these in order according to size?" he said loudly and slowly, as if I were hard of hearing and really stupid.

But who was being stupid? Didn't he know I couldn't grab the blocks? Of course I knew which block was bigger than the other. But I couldn't stack them if he paid me money! So I just took my arm and swept them all to the floor. They fell with a wooden clatter. I tried not to laugh as he picked them up. He breathed really hard as he reached for them.

Next, he held up glossy eight-by-ten cards with different colors painted on each one.

27

"Tell me when you see the color blue, Melody," he said in that voice that told me he thought this was all a waste of time.

When the blue card showed up, I pointed to it and made a noise. "Buh!" I said.

"Marvelous! Tremendous! Stupendous!" he shouted. He praised me like I had just passed the test to get into college. If I could have rolled my eyes, I would have.

Then he showed me green, so I kicked and made a noise, but my mouth can't make the *G* sound. The doctor looked disappointed.

He scribbled something on his clipboard, pulled out another stack of cards, then said, loudly, "I'm going to ask you some questions now, Melody. These might be hard, but do your best, okay?"

I just looked at him and waited while he placed the first set of cards in front of me.

"Number one. Which one of these is not like the others?"

Did he get this stuff from *Sesame Street*?

He showed me pictures of a tomato, a cherry, a round red balloon, and a banana. I know he was probably looking for the balloon as the answer, but that just seemed too easy. So I pointed to the banana because the first three were round and red, and the banana was not.

Dr. Hugely sighed and scribbled more

notes. "Number two," he said. He showed me four more cards. This time there were pictures of a cow, a whale, a camel, and an elephant. "Which animal gives birth to a calf?"

Now, I watch Animal Planet all the time. I know for a fact that *all* the animals he had pictured there had babies called a "calf." I thought doctors were supposed to be smart. What to do? I hit each picture slowly and carefully, then did it once more just to make sure he understood. I don't think he did.

I heard him mumble "cow" as he wrote more notes. It was clear he was giving up on me.

I noticed a copy of *Goodnight, Moon* on his bookshelf. I think it was written in Spanish. It was called *Buenas Noches, Luna.* That would have been fun to look at, but I had no way of telling him I'd like to see the book.

After watching *Sesame Street* and *Dora the Explorer* a million times, and sitting for hours watching the Spanish channels, I could understand quite a bit of Spanish if it was spoken slowly enough — and at least enough words to read the title of that book. He never thought to ask me about that, of course.

I knew the words and melodies of hundreds of songs — a symphony exploding inside my head with no one to hear it but me. But he never asked me about music.

I knew all the colors and shapes and animals that children my age were supposed to know, plus lots more. In my head I could count to one thousand — forward and backward. I could identify hundreds of words on sight. But all that was stuck inside.

Dr. Hugely, even though he had been to college for like, a million years, would never be smart enough to see inside of me. So I put on my handicapped face and took my mind back to last summer when Mom and I went to the zoo. I really liked the elephants, but talk about stink! Actually, Dr. Hugely sort of reminded me of one of them. My mom and the doctor had no idea why I was smiling as we rolled into the waiting room while he wrote up his evaluation of me. It didn't take long.

I'm always amazed at how adults assume I can't hear. They talk about me as if I'm invisible, figuring I'm too retarded to understand their conversation. I learn quite a bit this way. But this conversation was really awful. He didn't even try to soften the news for my mom, who, I'm sure, felt like she got hit by a truck.

He began by clearing his throat. "Mrs.

Brooks," he then said, "it is my opinion that Melody is severely brain-damaged and profoundly retarded."

Whoa! Even though I was only five, I had watched enough Easter Seals telethons to know this was bad. Really bad. I felt a thud in my gut.

My mom gasped, then said nothing for a full minute. Finally, she took a deep breath and protested quietly, "But I know she's bright. I can see it in her eyes."

"You love her. It's only normal to have wishful thinking," Dr. Hugely told her gently.

"No, she has a spark. More than that — a flame of real intelligence. I just know it," my mother insisted, sounding a little stronger.

"It takes time to accept the limitations of a beloved child. She has cerebral palsy, Mrs. Brooks."

"I know the *name* of her condition, Doctor," my mother said with ice in her voice. "But a person is so much more than the name of a diagnosis on a chart!"

Good try, Mom, I was thinking. But already her voice was losing its edge, melting into the mushiness of helplessness.

"She laughs at jokes," my mother told him, the ice in her voice replaced by desperation, "right at the punch line." Mom's voice faded. What she was saying sounded ridiculous, even to me, but I could see she just couldn't find the words to explain her gut feeling that I had some smarts stuck in here.

Dr. Hugely looked from her to me. He shook his head, then said, "You're lucky she has the ability to smile and laugh. But Melody will never be able to walk on her own or speak a single sentence. She will never be able to feed herself, take care of her own personal needs, or understand anything more than simple instructions. Once you accept that reality, you can deal with the future." That was just plain mean.

My mom hardly ever cries. But she did that day. She cried and cried and cried. Dr. Hugely had to give her a whole box of tissues. Both of them ignored me while she sobbed and he tried to find nice words to say to make her feel better. He didn't do a very good job.

Finally, he gave her options. "You and your husband have several decisions to make," he told Mom. "You can choose to keep her at home, or you can send her to a special school for the developmentally disabled. There aren't many choices here locally."

Where do they get those almost-pleasant-sounding phrases to describe kids like me?

Mom made a sound that could have been the mewing of a kitten. She was losing it.

Dr. Hugely continued. "You can also decide to put Melody in a residential facility where she can be cared for and kept comfortable."

He pulled out a colorful brochure with a smiling child in a wheelchair on the cover and handed it to Mom. I trembled as she took it.

"Let's see," the doctor said, "Melody is, ah, five now. That's a perfect age for her to learn to adjust to a new environment. You and your husband can get on with your lives without her as a burden. In time, her memories of you will fade."

I stared at Mom frantically. I didn't want to be sent away. Was I a burden? I never thought about it like that. Maybe it *would* be easier for them if I weren't around. I gulped. My hands got cold.

Mom wasn't looking at me. She was staring daggers at Dr. Hugely. She crumpled up the tissue she held and stood up. "Let me tell you something, Doctor. There is no way in heaven or hell that we will be sending Melody away to a nursing home!"

I blinked. Was this my mother? I blinked

again, and she was still there, right up in Dr. Hugely's face!

She wasn't finished. "You know what?" my mother said as she angrily hurled the brochure into the trash can. "I think you're cold and insensitive. I hope you never have a child with difficulties — you'd probably put it out with your trash!"

Dr. Hugely looked shocked.

"And what's more," she continued, "I think you're wrong — I know you are! Melody has more brains hidden in her head than you'll ever have, despite those fancy degrees from fancy schools you've got posted all over your walls!"

It was the doctor's turn to blink.

"You've got it easy — you have all your physical functions working properly. You never have to struggle just to be understood. You think you're smart because you have a medical degree?"

He was wise enough to keep his mouth shut and ashamed enough to lower his head.

Mom was on a roll. "You're not so intelligent, sir — you're just lucky! All of us who have all our faculties intact are just plain blessed. Melody is able to figure out things, communicate, and manage in a world where *nothing* works right for her. She's the one with the true intelligence!"

She marched out of his office then, rolling me swiftly through the thick doors. In the hall we did a quick fist bump — well, the best I could manage. My hands were no longer cold.

"I'm taking you right now and enrolling you at Spaulding Street Elementary School," she announced with determination as we headed back to the car. "Let's get busy!"

CHAPTER 5

I have been at Spaulding Street Elementary School for five years. It's very ordinary — filled with kids, just like the schools I see on television shows.

Kids who chase each other on the playground and run down the hall to get to their desks just before the bell rings.

Kids who slide on icy patches in the winter and stomp in puddles in the spring.

Kids who shout and push.

Kids who sharpen their pencils, go to the board to do math problems, and open their books to read a poem.

Kids who write their answers on notebook paper and stuff their homework into backpacks.

Kids who throw food at each other in the lunchroom while they sip on juice boxes.

Kids who sing in the choir, learn to play the violin, and take gymnastics or ballet or swimming lessons after school.

Kids who shoot baskets in the gym. Their conversation fills the halls as they make plans, make jokes, make friends.

Kids who, for the most part, ignore kids like me.

The "special needs" bus, as they call it, has a cool wheelchair lift built in the door, and it picks me up every morning in front of my house. When we get to school, the drivers take their time and make sure all the belts and buckles are tight before they lower all of us with walkers or wheelchairs or crutches or helmets down on the bus lift, one by one, to the ground. Then an aide will roll us, or help us walk, over to a waiting area.

When the weather is bright and sunny, we sit outside the school. I like to watch the "regular" kids as they play four-square while they wait for the bell to ring. They look like they're having so much fun. They ask one another to play, but no one's ever asked any of us. Not that we could, anyway, but it would be nice if somebody would say "Hi." I guess the four-square players must think we're all so backward that we don't care that we get treated like we're invisible.

I was so excited when Mom first enrolled me here. I thought I'd learn new things every day, but mostly it was simply something to do that took up time and got me out of the house. In second and third grades I probably learned more from the Sci Fi or Discovery Channels than I ever learned at school. My teachers were nice, most of the time, but they would've needed X-ray vision like Superman to see what was in my head.

I am in a special program with other children with what they call "disabilities." Our ages range from nine to eleven. Our "learning community" — what a joke — has been together since I started school. We never seem to move up and on like other classes. We just do what we did the year before, but with a new teacher. We don't even get a new classroom each year.

So the same kids I'm with now were together in second grade with a teacher named Mrs. Tracy. As third graders we suffered through Mrs. Billups, who could have got the award for worst teacher in the world. There are six self-contained learning communities in our wing of the building — children with various conditions, from preschoolers to kids who ought to be in high school by now.

Our classroom, room H-5, might be nice for babies, but give me a break! It's painted yellow and pink. One wall is covered with a sun with a happy face, a huge rainbow, and dozens of flowers — also with smiley faces. The other wall is painted with happy bunnies, kittens, and puppies. Bluebirds fly all over a sky with perfect white clouds. Even the birds are smiling. I'm almost eleven years old, and if I have to look at puppies in paradise one more day, I think I'll puke!

Ashley, the youngest in our group, actually does puke quite a bit. She's nine, but she could pass for three. She has the smallest wheelchair I've ever seen.

She's our fashion model. She is just plain beautiful — movie-star eyes; long, curly hair; and a tiny pixie nose. She looks like a doll that you see in a box on a shelf, except she's prettier. Her mother dresses her in a perfectly matching outfit every day. If she has on a pink shirt, she wears pink slacks, pink socks, and two tiny pink bows in her hair. Even her little fingernails have been done to match.

When we do what the teachers and therapists call "group" activities, it's hard for Ashley to participate. Her body is really stiff, and it's tough for her to reach or grab or hold anything.

Every Christmas they make the kids in H-5 decorate a stupid six-foot Styrofoam snowman. I don't know what the children in the regular classrooms get to do, but I know it's close to holiday time when whatever teacher we have that year pulls this thing out of a closet.

Mrs. Hyatt, the kindergarten teacher, loved that messed-up snowman, just three huge balls of yellowing Styrofoam, stuck together with pins and pipes.

"Let's decorate, children!" she said in her squeaky and annoying voice. "We are going to place decorations with Velcro or toothpicks or glue — whatever works — on Sydney, our H-5 holiday snowman!"

I don't know how old the snowman was at that point, but poor Sydney could not stand up straight. It leaned like a drunk who needed the wall to hold it up. Mrs. Hyatt gave us green snowflakes. Green? We were the dumb kids. I guess we weren't supposed to care. Brown garland. Stars in purple and pink.

"Do you like the snowman, Ashley?" Mrs. Hyatt asked her. It's almost impossible for Ashley to communicate because her body is so tight. Her "talking board" has just two words on it — *yes* and *no.* She turned her head slightly to the left for no. I bet she wished she could knock the thing down.

Compared to Ashley, Carl is huge. Even though he's just nine, he's got a special

40

wheelchair that's extra wide, and it takes two aides to lift him in and out of it. But he's good with his hands. He can move his own chair, and he can hold a pencil well enough to write his name. And stab a snowman.

Carl sticks pencils and rulers into the snowman's torso and pens into its head. Mrs. Hyatt used to clap her hands and say in her little squeaky voice, "Good job, Carl! So very creative!"

Carl would just laugh. He can talk, but only in very short sentences that usually have two parts. He has very strong opinions. "Snowman is dumb," he'd yell. "Very, very dumb."

I think he hates the snowman as much as I do. One year he pinned a diaper on the back and another on the front of the bottom third of the snowman. The teacher let them stay. Carl knows diapers.

When he poops in his pants, which is almost every day, the whole room smells like the monkey house at the zoo. The aides are so patient with him, though. They snap on their rubber gloves, clean him up, change his clothes — he always wears sweats — and sit him back in his chair. Those aides deserve medals. We're not an easy bunch.

Maria, who has Down syndrome, is ten.

She *loves* Christmas and Easter and Valentine's Day and Earth Day — it doesn't matter. If it's a holiday, Maria is ready to celebrate. She's wide around the middle, a little like our snowman, but Maria talks all the time. She's fun to be around, even though she insists on calling me "Melly-Belly."

Every year when it's time to bring out the ancient snowman, Maria jumps and cheers with real excitement. I'm pretty sure she's the only kid in our class who truly likes it.

"It's time for Sydney the Snowman!" she gasps. "Can I put his hat on? Please? Please? Can I give him my red scarf? Sydney will love my red scarf!"

Mrs. Hyatt and every teacher after her always let Maria take charge of the green paper cutout candy canes and the purple-striped stars cut from wrapping paper. Maria kisses each decoration before attaching it with Velcro to the snowman. She hugs Sydney each afternoon before she goes home. And she cries when it's time to put Sydney away each year.

Even though she has trouble figuring out complicated stuff, Maria understands people and how they feel. "Why are you sad today, Melly-Belly?" she asked me one morning a couple of years ago. How could she have known that my goldfish had died the day before? I let her give me a big hug, and I felt better.

If Maria is our hugger, Gloria is our rocker. She rocks for hours in the corner under one of the dumb smiling flowers. The teachers are always trying to coax her out, but she wraps her arms around herself like she's cold and keeps on rocking. She's autistic, I think. She can walk perfectly well, and she talks when she has something to say. It's always worth listening to.

"Snowman makes me shiver," she blurted out one day when the classroom was surprisingly quiet. Then she curled up in her corner and said nothing else until it was time to go home. She's never added one decoration to our snowman, but she does uncurl and seem to relax when a teacher puts on a CD of holiday music.

Willy Williams — yes, that's his real name — is eleven. I'm not sure what his diagnosis is. He yodels, like one of those Swiss people in a mountain-climbing commercial. He makes other noises, too — whistles and grunts and shrieks. He's never, ever quiet and never completely still. I sometimes wonder if he makes all those noises and movements in his sleep.

When Sydney the Snowman comes out of

whatever box they keep him in during most of the year, the teacher has to keep Willy at a distance because he'll knock the wobbly thing down. Willy's not trying to be mean — it's just that his arms and legs are in constant motion. He can't help it.

Mrs. Hyatt was the first teacher to witness Sydney topple over. "Why don't you add this bright pink bow to our snowman?" she had squeaked to Willy that first year.

All arms and movement, Willy tried, but the stupid pink bow went in one direction and poor Sydney went in the other. Three separate balls rolled across the room. Willy shrieked and whistled. I think I saw him smile as well.

Now, if Mrs. Hyatt had given Willy a baseball to glue to the snowman, it would have been placed more carefully. Willy *loves* baseball.

Our first-grade teacher, Mr. Gross, liked to play guessing games. Willy just burbled if the questions were about butterflies or boats, but watch out if the question was about baseball. He'd screech out the right answer before the yelps and bellows took over.

"Who was the first baseball player to hit sixty home runs in one season?" Mr. Gross asked.

44

"Babe Ruth!" Then a screech.

"Who broke Babe Ruth's record of seven hundred fourteen home runs?"

"Hank Aaron!" Whooping noises.

"And who is the all-time hit king?" Mr. Gross seemed to be astonished at Willy's knowledge.

"Pete Rose! Four-two-five-six. Eeek!"

"And who holds the lifetime touchdown record?"

Silence. Not even a squeak. Willy doesn't bother with football. Or snowmen.

Sometimes when I look at Willy, though, I get the feeling that he really wishes he could be still and silent. I watch him as he closes his eyes, frowns up his face, and concentrates. For just a few minutes he's quiet. He takes a deep breath, like a swimmer coming up for air. When he opens his eyes, the noises start all over. And then he always looks sad.

Jill uses a walker because her left foot drags a little as she walks. She's thin and pale and very quiet. When Sydney comes out for the season, Jill's eyes are almost blank. It's like the light has been clicked off. She cries a lot. Mr. Gross used to put decorations in her hand and try to make it easy for her to join the activity, but it was like helping a store mannequin. I heard an aide say she was in a car accident when she was a baby. I think that's awful — to start out okay, then lose the ability to do stuff.

Freddy, who's almost twelve, is the oldest in our group. He uses an electric wheelchair. He loves that thing. He tells me every chance he gets, "Freddy go zoom! Freddy go zoom!" He grins, pretends he's putting on a helmet, then he pushes the controller to its max position and takes off across the room. Of course, his speed control has two settings — slow and slower. But to Freddy, he's at the racetrack.

He zooms his electric chair around the raggedy old snowman, tossing Velcroed stars and bells at it, asking, "Snowman go zoom zoom?"

Well, after Willy sent it flying, and Carl tried to stab it with pencils, I guess it was a fair question! Every year Freddy adds his own touches to the snowman — NASCAR and NASA decals like the ones on his chair. If you ask Freddy what date it is, he can't tell you. But if you want to know who won the Daytona 500, Freddy will know.

And then there's me.

I hate the stupid snowman. But I toss tinsel at it like they ask me to. It's easier than trying to explain.

I have a large Plexiglas tray that fastens to

46

the arms of my chair. It serves as a food tray as well as a communication board. When I was younger, Mom pasted dozens of words on it, but I was still limited to only a handful of common nouns, verbs, and adjectives, some names, and a bunch of smiley faces. There are also a few necessary phrases, like, *I need to go to the bathroom, please* and *I'm hungry,* but most people — even little kids — need to say more than that in a day. Duh!

I've got *please* and *thank you, yes, no,* and *maybe* close together on the right-hand side. On the left are the names of people in my family, kids in my class, and teachers. The name "Sydney" is not included.

There's an alphabet strip at the top, so I can spell out words, and a row of numbers under that, so I can count or say how many or talk about time. But for the majority of my life, I've had the communication tools of a little kid on my board. It's no wonder everybody thinks I'm retarded.

I hate that word, by the way. *Retarded.*

I like all the kids in room H-5, and I understand their situations better than anybody, but there's nobody else like *me.* It's like I live in a cage with no door and no key. And I have no way to tell someone how to get me out.

Oh, wait! I forgot about Mrs. V!

CHAPTER 6

Mrs. Violet Valencia lives next door to us. Violets are purple, and Valencia oranges are, well, orange! Purple oranges are just plain unusual, and so is she. She's a big woman — about six feet tall, with the biggest hands I've ever seen. They're huge! I bet she could put a full-size basketball in each of her palms and still have room left over. If Mrs. V is, well, like a tree, then my mom is a twig next to her.

I was about two years old when I first started hanging out at Mrs. V's house. Mom and Dad hardly left me with anybody at first, but sometimes their work schedules overlapped, and they needed a third person to help out. Mom said Mrs. V was the very first visitor when I first came home from the hospital, the first person to just pick me up like any other baby. A lot of my parents' friends had been scared to even touch me, but not Mrs. V!

Mrs. V wears huge, flowing dresses — must be miles of material in those things — all in crazy color combinations. Bubble-gum pink, with fire-engine red, with peachy sherbet, with bright cinnamon. And all shades of orange and purple, of course. She told me she makes the dresses herself. I guess she'd have to. I have never seen anything like them in any store in the mall. Or in a hospital, either.

Mrs. V and Mom used to work together as nurses at the hospital. Mom told me the children there had been crazy about her. She wore the same bright outfits in the preemie ward, the kids' cancer ward, the children's burn unit. "Color brings life and hope to these children!" she'd announce boldly, daring anybody to disagree. I guess nobody did.

I remember sitting on Mrs. V's porch that very first time. Mom and Dad looked concerned, but Mrs. V held me tightly and bounced me on her knees. She must have a hidden microphone under those flowing clothes — she has one of those voices that can make anybody shut up, turn, and listen.

"Of course I'll watch Melody," she'd said with certainty.

"Well, Melody is, well, you know, really special," Dad said hesitantly.

"*All* kids are special," Mrs. V had replied with authority. "But this one has hidden superpowers. I'd love to help her find them."

"We can't possibly pay you what this is worth to us," Dad began.

Mrs. V had shrugged and said with a smile, "I'll appreciate whatever you can give me."

My dad looked sheepish. "Well, thanks. And I'll get that ramp finished this weekend. I just need to make one more trip to the lumberyard."

"Now, *that* will be a big help," Mrs. V had said with a nod.

"Melody can be a handful," Mom had warned.

Mrs. V lifted me into the air. "I've got big hands."

"We want her to reach her highest potential," Dad added.

"Oh, gag me!" Mrs. V said, startling him. "Don't get bogged down in all those touchy-feely words and phrases you read in books on disabled kids. Melody is a child who can learn and will learn if she sticks with me!"

Dad looked embarrassed. But then he grinned. "Bring her back in twenty years."

"You'll have her back home by supper-time!"

So most workdays I'd end up at Mrs. Valencia's place for a couple of hours until Mom or Dad could get home. When I got older, I went over to Mrs. V's every afternoon after school. I don't know how much they paid her, but it couldn't have been enough.

From the very beginning, Mrs. Valencia gave me no sympathy. Instead of sitting me in the special little chair my parents had bought for me, she plopped me on my back in the middle of the floor on a large, soft quilt. The first time she did that, I looked up at her like she was crazy. I cried. I screeched. She ignored me, walked away, and flipped on her CD player. Loud marching band music blared through the room. I liked it.

Then she came back and put my favorite toy — a rubber monkey — a few inches from my head. I wanted that monkey. It squeaked when you touched it. But it may as well have been a million miles away. I was on my back, stuck like a turtle. I screamed louder.

Mrs. V sat down on the quilt. "Turn over, Melody," she said quietly. Sometimes she can make her voice really soft.

I was so shocked, I stopped yelling. I couldn't turn over. Didn't she know that? Was she nuts?

She wiped my nose with a tissue. "You can turn yourself over, Melody. I know you understand every word I say to you, and I know you can do this. Now roll!"

Actually, I'd never bothered to try very hard to roll anywhere. I'd fallen off the sofa a couple of times, and it hurt, so I usually just waited for Mom or Dad to move me to a comfortable position.

"Look at how you're lying. You're already on your side — halfway there. Use all that screaming and hollering energy you've got to take you to another position. Toss your right arm over and concentrate!"

So I did. I strained. I reached. I tried so hard, I farted! Mrs. V cracked up. But slowly, slowly, I felt my body rolling to the right. And then, unbelievably, *plop!* I was on my stomach. I was so proud of myself, I screeched.

"I told you so," Mrs. V said, victory in her voice. "Now go get that monkey!"

I knew better than to protest. So I reached for it. The monkey was now only two inches from my hand. I tried to scoot. My legs kept doing the opposite of what my head wanted them to do. I wiggled. I grabbed a fistful of the quilt and pulled. The monkey got closer!

"You're a smart little cookie," Mrs. V told me.

I gave the quilt another tug, and finally, gradually, I had the monkey in my hand. I clutched it, and it squeaked as if it were glad to see me. I grinned and made it squeak again and again.

"After that workout, you must be hungry," she said. She fed me a vanilla milk shake first, then my vegetables and noodles. Mrs. Valencia *always* serves dessert first. And I always eat all my food — the healthy part, and the yummy part, too. It's our secret.

Mrs. V is the only person who lets me drink soda. Coke. Sprite. Tahitian Treat. I love the nose-tickling burp. Mom and Dad mostly give me milk and juice. Mello Yello is my favorite. Mrs. V even started calling me that.

At Mrs. V's house I learned to scoot and then to crawl. I'd never win a baby-crawling contest, but by the time I was three, I had learned to get across a room. She made me figure out how to flip myself over from front to back and back to front again. She was tough on me. She let me fall out of my wheelchair onto pillows so I could learn how best to catch myself.

"Suppose somebody forgets to fasten that seat belt of yours," she said in that voice that sounded like she was chewing gravel. "You better know what to do, or you'll bust your head wide open."

I didn't want a busted head, so we practiced. She'd send me back home, tell Mom I had a good dinner and a good poop — I have no idea why parents think that's so important — then wink at me. I was like her secret mission.

Once I started school, however, I discovered I had a much bigger problem than just falling out of my chair. I needed words. How was I supposed to learn anything if I couldn't talk? How was I supposed to answer questions? Or ask questions?

I knew a lot of words, but I couldn't read a book. I had a million thoughts in my head, but I couldn't share them with anybody. On top of that, people didn't really expect the kids in H-5 to learn much anyway. It was driving me crazy!

I couldn't have been much more than six when Mrs. V figured out what I needed. One afternoon after school, after a snack of ice cream with caramel sauce, she flipped through the cable channels and stopped at a documentary about some guy named Stephen Hawking.

Now I'm interested in almost anything that has a wheelchair in it. Duh! I even like the Jerry Lewis telethon! Turns out Stephen Hawking has something called ALS, and he can't walk or talk, and he's probably the smartest man in the world, and *everybody* knows it! That is so cool.

I bet he gets really frustrated sometimes.

After the show went off, I got real quiet.

"He's like you, sort of, isn't he?" Mrs. V asked.

I pointed to **yes** on my board, then pointed to **no**.

"I don't follow you." She scratched her head.

I pointed to **need** on my board, then to **read. Need/ read. Need/read.**

"I know you can read lots of words, Melody," Mrs. V said.

I pointed again. **More.** I could feel tears coming. **More. More. More.**

"Melody, if you had to choose, which would you rather be able to do — walk or talk?"

Talk. I pointed to my board. I hit the word again and again. **Talk. Talk. Talk.**

I have *so* much to say.

So Mrs. V made it her new mission to give me language. She ripped all the words off my communication board and started from scratch. She made the new words smaller, so more could fit. Every single space on my talking board got filled with names and pictures of people in my life, questions I might need to ask, and a big variety of nouns and verbs and adjectives, so I could actually compose something that looked like a sentence! I could ask, *Where is my book bag?* or say, *Happy Birthday, Mom,* just by pointing with my thumb.

I have magic thumbs, by the way. They work perfectly. The rest of my body is sort of like a coat with the buttons done up in the wrong holes. But my thumbs came out with no flaws, no glitches. Just my thumbs. Go figure.

Every time Mrs. V would add new words, I learned them quickly, used them in sentences, and was hungry for more. I wanted to READ!

So she made flash cards.

Pink for nouns.

Blue for verbs.

Green for adjectives.

Piles and piles of words I learned to read. Little words, like *fish* and *dish* and *swish.* I like rhyming words — they're easy to remember. It's like a "buy one, get the rest free" sale at the mall.

I learned big words, like *caterpillar* and *mosquito,* and words that follow crazy rules, like *knock* and *gnome.* I learned all the days of the week, months of the year, all the planets, oceans, and continents. Every single day I learned new words. I sucked them in and gobbled them up like they were Mrs. V's cherry cake.

And then she would stretch out the cards on the floor, position me on a big pillow so I could reach them, and I'd push the cards into sentences with my fists. It was like stringing the beads of a necklace together to make something really cool.

I liked to make her laugh, so I'd put the words into wacky order sometimes.

The blue fish will run away. He does not want to be dinner.

She also taught me words for all the music I heard at home. I learned to tell the difference between Beethoven and Bach, between a sonata and a concerto. She'd pick a selection on a CD, then ask me the composer.

Mozart. I'd point to the correct card from the choices she'd set in front of me. Then I'd point to the color blue on my board.

"Huh?" she asked.

When she played a selection from Bach, I'd point to the correct composer, then once again touch the color blue on my board. I also touched purple.

She looked confused. I searched around for the right words to explain what I meant. I wanted her to understand that music was

58

colorful when I heard it. I finally realized that even Mrs. V couldn't figure out everything in my head.

We kept going.

Sometimes she'd play hip-hop music, sometimes oldies. Music, and the colors it produced, flowed around her as easily as her clothing.

Mrs. V took me outside in all kinds of weather. One day she actually let me sit outside in the rain. It was steaming hot, and I was sticky and irritable. It must have been about ninety degrees outside. We were sitting on her porch, watching the storm clouds gather. She told me the names of all the clouds and made up stories about them. I knew that later she'd have the names of every kind of cloud on word cards for me.

"Big old Nimbus up there — he's black and powerful and can blow all the other clouds out of the sky. He wants to marry Miss Cumulus Cloud, but she's too soft and pretty to be bothered with such a scary guy. So he gets mad and makes storms," she told me.

Finally, old Nimbus got his way, and the rain came down around me and Mrs. V. It rained so hard, I couldn't see past the porch. The wind blew, and the wet coolness of the rain washed over us. It felt so good.

A small leak on Mrs. V's porch let a few drops of rain fall on my head. I laughed out loud.

Mrs. V gave me a funny look, then hopped up. "You want to feel it all?" she asked.

I nodded my head. *Yes, yes, yes.*

She rolled me down the ramp Dad had built, both of us getting wetter every second. She stopped when we got to the grass, and we let the rain drench us. My hair, my clothes, my eyes and arms and hands. Wet. Wet. Wet. It was awesome. The rain was warm, almost like bathwater. I laughed and laughed.

Eventually, Mrs. V rolled me back up the ramp and into the house, where she dried me off, changed my clothes, and gave me a cup of chocolate milk. She dried off my chair, and by the time Dad came to pick me up, the rain had stopped and everything was dry once more.

I dreamed of chocolate clouds all night.

CHAPTER 7

When I sleep, I dream. And in my dreams I can do anything. I get picked first on the playground for games. I can run so fast! I take gymnastics, and I never fall off the balance beam. I know how to square-dance, and I'm good at it. I call my friends on the phone, and we talk for hours. I whisper secrets. I sing.

When I wake up in the morning, it's always sort of a letdown as reality hits me. I have to be fed and dressed so I can spend another long day in the happy-face room at Spaulding Street School.

Along with the assortment of teachers we've had in room H-5, there have been more classroom aides than I can count. These aides — usually one guy to help with the boys and one lady to help with the girls — do stuff like take us to the bathroom (or change diapers on kids like Ashley and Carl), feed us at lunch, wheel us where we need to go, wipe mouths, and give hugs. I don't think they get paid very much, because they never stay very long. But they should get a million dollars. What they do is really hard, and I don't think most folks get that.

It's even hard to keep good teachers for us. I guess I don't blame them for leaving, because, like I said, we're a tough bunch to handle sometimes.

But once in a while we get a good one. After squeaky Mrs. Hyatt for kindergarten and game-show Mr. Gross for first grade, Mrs. Tracy breezed into our room for second grade.

She figured out I liked books, so she got some earphones and hooked me up with audiobooks on CD. She started with baby stuff, like Dr. Seuss, which my father and I had read when I was two, so after I tossed those on the floor a couple of times, instead of punishing me, she figured out I needed something better.

I listened to all of the Baby-Sitters Club books and those goofy Goosebumps books. She asked me questions after each book, and I got every single question right. Things like, "Which of these helped to solve the mystery?" Then she'd show me a pebble, a starfish, and an ink pen. The pebble, of course. She'd cheer after we'd gone through the questions and then hook me up to another book. That year I listened to all the books by Beverly Cleary and all the books about those boxcar kids. It was awesome.

The next year it all unraveled. I know teachers are supposed to write notes to the next teacher in line so they know what to expect, but either Mrs. Tracy didn't do it or Mrs. Billups, our third-grade teacher, didn't read them.

Mrs. Billups started every morning by playing her favorite CD. I hated it. "Old MacDonald Had a Farm," "Twinkle, Twinkle, Little Star," "The Itsy-Bitsy Spider" — all sung by children who could not sing, the type of music grown-ups think is all kinds of cute, but it's awful!

Mrs. Billups put it on — at full volume — every single morning. Over and over and over. No wonder we were always in a bad mood.

Once she had the tin-pan band on, Mrs. Billups went over the alphabet. Every single day. With *third* graders.

"Now, children, this is an 'A.' How many of you can say 'A'? Good!"

She'd smile and say "good" even if nobody in the class responded.

I wondered if she would teach able-bodied

third graders the same way. Probably not. The more I thought about it, the angrier I got.

"Now let's move on to 'B.' This is the letter 'B.' Let's all say 'B.' Good!"

Again to silence. She didn't seem to care. I glanced with longing at the books on tape and the earphones, which had been shoved into a corner.

One day I guess I'd had enough. Mrs. Billups had expanded from saying the letters to making the sound of each one.

"Buh!" she said loudly, spitting a little as she did. " 'Buh' is the sound of the letter 'B.' Let's all say 'buh' together, children."

Then Maria, who is always in a good mood, started throwing crayons. Willy began to babble. And I bellowed.

I may not be able to make clear sounds, but I can make a *lot* of noise.

I screamed because I hated stuff that was just plain stupid.

I screeched because I couldn't talk and tell her to shut up!

And that made me cry because I'd *never* be able to tell *anybody* what I was really thinking.

So I screamed and yelled and shrieked. I cried like a two-year-old. I would not stop.

Then my tornado explosion took over. I

flailed and jerked and basically spazzed out. I kicked so hard that my shoes popped out of the foot straps on my chair. That made me tilt to one side, and I screamed even louder.

Mrs. Billups didn't know what to do. She tried to calm me down, but I didn't *want* to be calmed. Even the aides couldn't stop me. Jill and Maria started to cry. Even Ashley, dressed all in yellow that day, looked upset. Freddy spun his chair around in circles, glancing sideways at me fearfully. Carl hollered for lunch. Then he pooped in his pants again. The whole class was out of control. And I kept screeching.

The teacher called Mrs. Anthony, the principal, whose eyes got wide as she opened our door. She took one look at the situation and said tersely, "Call her mother." She could not have left more quickly.

A moment later the teacher had my mother on the phone. "Mrs. Brooks, this is Melody's teacher, Anastasia Billups. Can you come to the school right away?"

I knew my mother had to be worried. Was I sick? Bleeding? Dead?

"No, she's not ill. She's fine, we think," Mrs. Billups was saying in her most professional-sounding teacher voice. "We just can't get her to stop screaming. She's

65

got the whole class in an uproar."

I could picture my mother on the other end of the line trying to figure out what was going on. Luckily, it was her day off. I knew she'd be there in a few minutes. So I gradually calmed down and finally shut up. The other kids quieted down as well, like somebody had clicked the off switch.

"Old MacDonald" continued to play.

My mother arrived faster than I thought possible. When I saw her jeans and dirty sweatshirt, I realized she'd dropped everything and jumped in the car. She ran over to me and asked what was wrong.

I took a few deep, shuddering breaths, then I pointed to the alphabet on my talking board and screeched some sounds of frustration.

"This is about the alphabet?" my mother asked.

Yes. I pointed, then pounded on the answer.

She turned to Mrs. Billups. "What were you working on before all the screaming started?"

Mrs. Billups replied, in that superior tone that teachers dressed in nice red business suits use when they're talking to mothers with dirty shirts on, "We were reviewing the alphabet, of course. The sound of the letter

66

'B,' if I recall. I always start with the basics. These children need constant review because they don't retain information like the rest of us."

My mother was getting the picture. "So you were going over the ABCs?"

"Correct."

"It's February."

"I beg your pardon?"

"School started in August. You haven't gotten past the letter 'B' in six months?" Mom was balling and unballing her fists. I've never seen my mother hit anything, but when I see her doing that, I always wonder if she might.

"Who are you to tell me how to run my class?" the teacher asked angrily.

"And who are you to bore these children with mindless activities?" my mother snapped back.

"How dare you!" the teacher gasped.

"I dare anything for my daughter," Mom replied, her voice dangerous, "and for the rest of these children!"

"You don't understand —," the teacher began.

Mom interrupted her. "No, Mrs. Billups, it is *you* who does not understand!" Mom looked like she was trying to calm herself down, because she then said, "Look. Have

67

you ever said to yourself, 'If they show that stupid commercial on TV one more time, I think I'll just scream'?"

Mrs. Billups nodded slowly.

"Or, 'If I have to sit five more minutes in this traffic jam, I'll simply explode'?"

"Yes, I suppose," she admitted.

"Well, I think that's what happened to Melody. She said to herself, 'If I have to go over those letters one more time, I'll just scream.' So she did. I really don't blame her, do you?"

Mrs. Billups looked from my mother to me. "I guess not, now that you explain it that way," Mrs. Billups finally said, her voice now as calm as my mother's.

"Melody knows her alphabet, all the sounds of all the letters, and *hundreds* of words on sight. She can add and subtract numbers in her head. We discussed all this at our last parent conference, didn't we?" I could tell my mother was trying to control her temper.

"I thought you were exaggerating," the teacher said. "Parents are not always realistic when it comes to these children."

"If you call them 'these children' one more time, *I* might scream," my mother warned.

"But Melody *does* have mental and physical limitations," Mrs. Billups argued, trying to put Mom in her place, I guess. "You have to learn to accept that."

And the fire was back. "Melody can't walk. Melody can't talk. But she is *extremely* intelligent! And *you* better learn to accept *that*!" Mom spat out.

The teacher backed up an inch or two.

"Didn't you read her records from last year?" Mom demanded. "Melody loves listening to the books on tape."

"I try to approach each child with an open mind and not be influenced by other teachers. All the records are in a box someplace."

"Maybe you should find that box," my mother said, her lips tight.

"Well, I never!" Mrs. Billups countered.

"Maybe that's your problem!" Mom replied with a grin. Then she tilted her head and turned toward the CD player. "Oh, one more thing. May I see that wonderful CD you're playing?"

"Of course," Mrs. Billups said, smiling a little. "The children love this."

"Do they?" Mom asked.

The teacher lifted the disc from the player.

Twinkle, twinkle, silence.

Willy sighed out loud.

Mom took the CD, dug down in her purse for a moment, gave Mrs. Billups a five-

69

dollar bill, and deftly snapped the disc in half.

"That music was cruel and unusual punishment!"

Freddy and Maria cheered.

Gloria whispered, "Thank you."

For a moment I almost felt sorry for Mrs. Billups. She looked so confused. She just didn't get it.

Mom walked over to the sink in our room, turned on the warm water, and soaked a stack of paper towels under the faucet. She came back to me and gently wiped my face with the warm, soggy wad. Nothing had ever felt so soothing. She then brushed my hair, adjusted the straps and buckles on my chair, gave me a quick hug, and went home.

Mrs. Billups quit her job after spring break, so we ended up with a series of subs till the end of the year. I think she had figured it would be easy to work with people who were dumber than she was.

She was wrong.

CHAPTER 8

For a long time it was just me, my mom and dad, and my goldfish, Ollie. I was five years old when I got him, and I had him for almost two years before he died. I guess that's old for a goldfish. Nobody knew Ollie's name but me, but that's okay. Ollie had been a prize from a carnival Dad had taken me to, and I think Ollie's life was worse than mine.

He lived in a small bowl on the table in my room. The bottom of the bowl was covered with tiny pink rocks, and a fake plastic log sat wedged in the rocks. I guess it was supposed to look like something from under the sea, but I don't think there are any lakes or oceans that really have rocks that color.

Ollie spent all day long swimming around that small bowl, ducking through the fake log, and then swimming around again. He always swam in the same direction. The only time he'd change his course was when Mom dropped a few grains of fish food into his bowl each morning and evening. I'd watch him gobble the food, then poop it out, then swim around and around once again. I felt sorry for him.

At least I got to go outside and to the store and to school. Ollie just swam in a circle all day. I wondered if fish ever slept. But any time I woke up in the middle of the night, Ollie was still swimming, his little mouth opening and closing like was he trying to say something.

One day when I was about seven, Ollie jumped out of his bowl. I had been listening to music on the radio — Mom had finally figured out I liked the country-western station — and I was in a good mood. The music was sounding orangey and yellowish as I listened, and the faint whiff of lemons seemed to surround me. I felt real mellow as I watched Ollie do his thing round and round his bowl.

But suddenly, for no reason I could figure, Ollie dove down to the bottom of his bowl, rushed to the top, and hurled himself right out of the bowl. He landed on the table. He gasped and flopped, and I'm sure he was surprised he couldn't breathe. His eyes bulged, and the gills on his side pulsed with effort.

I didn't know what to do. He'd die without water — really fast. So I screamed. Mom was downstairs, or maybe outside getting the mail, but she didn't come right away. I screamed again. Louder. I cried out. I yelled. I screeched. Ollie continued to flop and gasp, looking more desperate. Ollie needed water.

I howled once more, but Mom didn't come running. Where could she be? I knew I had to do something, so I reached over to the table and stretched out my arm. I could just barely touch Ollie's bowl. I figured if I could get the fish wet, at least a little bit, I might be able to save him. I hooked my fingers on the edge of the fishbowl, and I pulled. Water splashed everywhere — all over the table, the carpet, me, and Ollie. He seemed to flop a little less for a second or two.

And I kept wailing. Finally, I heard my mother thundering up the stairs. When she came through the door, she took one look at the mess and the dying goldfish and shouted, "Melody! What have you done? Why did you knock over the fishbowl? Don't you know a fish can't live without water?"

Of course I knew that. I'm not stupid. Why did she think I'd been screeching and calling for her?

She scurried over to the mess, scooped up Ollie, and gently placed him back in the bowl. Then she ran to the bathroom, and I heard her running water. But I knew it was too late.

Either because of the time out of the bowl or because the bathroom water wasn't the right temperature, Ollie didn't survive.

Mom came back in and scolded me once more. "Your goldfish didn't make it, Melody. I don't get it. Why would you do that to the poor little fish? He was happy in his little world."

I wondered if maybe Ollie wasn't so happy after all. Maybe he was sick and tired of that bowl and that log and that circle. Maybe he just couldn't take it anymore. I feel like that sometimes.

There was no way I could explain to Mom what had happened. I really *had* tried to save Ollie's life. I just looked away from Mom. She was angry, and I was too. If she hadn't been so slow, Ollie might have made it. I didn't want her to see me cry.

She cleaned up the mess with a sigh and left me with my music and an empty spot on my table. The colors had vanished.

It was a long time before I was ready for another pet. But on my eighth birthday my father brought a big box into the house. He seemed to have trouble holding on to it. When he set it on the floor in front of me, out exploded a flash of wriggling gold fun. A puppy! A golden retriever puppy! I shrieked and kicked with joy. A puppy!

The clumsy little dog raced around the room, sniffing in every corner. I watched her every move — loving her right away. After exploring every table leg and piece of furniture, the puppy stopped, made sure all of us were watching, then squatted and peed right there on the carpet! Mom yelled, but only a little. That's when the dog knew she was in charge.

She checked out Dad's bare toes, but she stayed away from Mom, who was trying to soak the spot out of the rug with paper towels and that spray stuff she uses in the kitchen. Finally, the puppy circled my wheelchair around and around, like she was trying to figure it out. She sniffed it, sniffed my legs and feet, looked at me for a minute, then jumped right up onto my lap like she'd done it a million times. I barely breathed, not wanting to disturb her. Then, wow, wow, wow, she turned around three times and made herself comfortable. I think she made a noise like a sigh of satisfaction. I know I did. I stroked her soft back and head as gently as I could.

I was the one who named her. Mom and Dad kept suggesting dumb names like Fuzzy and Coffee, but I knew as soon as I saw her what her name should be. I pointed to the bowl on the table, which held my most favorite, favorite candies — butterscotch caramel. They're soft enough to melt in my mouth, so I don't have to chew, and oh, are they delicious!

"You want to call her Candy?" Dad asked. I shook my head no, gently, so the sleeping puppy wouldn't wake up.

"Caramel?" Mom asked.

I shook my head once more.

"Why don't we call her Stinky?" Dad suggested with a grin. Mom and I just glared at him. I continued to point to the candy dish.

Finally, Mom said, "I know! You want to call her Butterscotch?"

I wanted to shriek, but I forced myself to stay calm. I tried real hard not to do anything that would knock the puppy off my lap. "Uh," I said softly as I continued to stroke the dog's silky fur. I didn't know that anything could be so soft. And she was all mine. It was the best birthday I ever had.

Butterscotch sleeps at the foot of my bed every night. It's like she read the book on what a great dog ought to do: bark only when a stranger is at the door, never pee or poop in the house (she got over that puppy stuff), and keep Melody happy. Butterscotch doesn't care that I can't talk to her — she knows I love her. She just gets it.

One day, a few months after I got her, I fell out of my wheelchair. It happens. Mom had given me lunch, taken me to the toilet, and wheeled me back into my room. Butterscotch trotted behind — never in the way, just close by me all the time. Mom popped in a DVD for me and made sure my hands were properly positioned so I could rewind and fast-forward the film. She didn't notice my seat belt wasn't fastened, and neither did I.

She traveled up and down the stairs doing several loads of laundry — I'm awfully messy — and I guess she had started fixing dinner. The rich aroma of simmering tomato sauce floated up the stairs. Mom knows I love spaghetti.

She peeked her head in to check on me and said, "I'm going to lie down for a couple of minutes, Melody. Are you okay for a few?"

I nodded and pointed my arm toward the

door to tell her to go ahead. My movie was getting good anyway. Butterscotch sat curled next to my chair; she'd outgrown my lap. So Mom blew me a kiss and closed the door.

I was watching something I'd seen a million times — *The Wizard of Oz.* I think most people in the world can quote sections of that movie — no extra brains required — because it's one of the movies that gets played over and over again on cable channels. But I know every single word in it. I know what Dorothy will say before she even opens her mouth. "I don't think we're in Kansas anymore, Toto!" It makes me smile. I've never been to Kansas or Oz or anywhere more than a few miles away from home.

Even though I knew it was coming, when the movie got to the part where the Tin Man does that stiff little dance to the music of "If I Only Had a Heart," I cracked up. I laughed so hard, I jerked forward in my chair and found myself facedown on the floor.

Butterscotch jumped up immediately, sniffing me and making sure I wasn't hurt. I was fine, but I couldn't get back up in my chair. Worse, I was going to miss the part where the Cowardly Lion gets smacked on the nose by Dorothy. I wondered how long

Mom's nap would last.

I didn't scream like that time Ollie had jumped out of the bowl. I wasn't upset, just a little uncomfortable. I tried to flip over, but I couldn't from the position I had landed in. If I could have seen the television from where I had fallen, I might have been okay on the floor for a little while. Butterscotch makes a great pillow.

But Butterscotch went to the closed door and scratched. I could hear her claws ripping at the wood. Dad wouldn't be happy when he saw that. But Mom didn't come. So Butterscotch barked — first a couple of tentative yips, then louder and more urgent. Finally, she jumped up and threw her whole body against the door, making loud thuds. She'd bark, then thud. Bark, then thud. Mom couldn't ignore all that racket.

I'm sure it was only a few minutes, but it seemed like longer. Mom came to the door, looking groggy. Her hair was all messed up. "What's going on in here?" she began. Then she saw me. "Oh! Melody, baby! Are you okay?" She ran to me, sat down on the floor, and lifted me onto her lap.

She checked everything — my arms and legs, my back, my face, my scalp, even my tongue. I wanted to tell her I was fine. All she needed to do was put me back in my chair, but she had to do the Mom thing and double-check.

"Butterscotch, you're a good, good girl!" she said as she petted the dog and hugged me tight. "Doubles on the dog food to-night!"

I'm sure Butterscotch would have pre-ferred a nice thick bone instead, but she can't talk either, so both my dog and I get what they give us. Mom carefully put me back in my chair and made sure my seat belt was latched correctly. Butterscotch curled up right in front of me, making sure, I guess, that if I slid out again, she'd be there to soften the fall. That dog is amazing.

Mom restarted the video from the begin-ning, but somehow that yellow brick road had lost some of its magic glow. Nobody *really* gets wishes granted by the Great Oz.

As I watched, I wondered if *I* were blown to Oz with *my* dog, what would we ask the wizard for?

Hmmm. Brains? I've got plenty.

Courage? Butterscotch is scared of noth-ing!

A heart? We've got lots of heart, me and my pup.

So what would I ask for? I'd like to sing like the Cowardly Lion and dance like the Tin Man. Neither one of them did those things very well, but that would be good enough for me.

CHAPTER 9

When I was eight, things changed.

I think I knew Mom was going to have a baby even before she did. She smelled different, like new soap. Her skin felt softer and warmer.

She picked me up out of bed one morning, then almost let me fall back on the mattress. "Whew!" she said. "You're getting awfully heavy, Melody. I'm going to have to start lifting weights!" Her forehead had broken out in sweat.

I don't think I'd gained any weight. It was Mom who was different. She sat down on the chair next to my bed for a few minutes, then suddenly ran out of the room. I heard her throwing up in the bathroom. She came back a few minutes later, looking pale. Her breath smelled like mouthwash. "I must have eaten something funky," she mumbled as she got me dressed. But I think she knew even then. I bet she was scared.

When Mom finally figured it out, she sat down with me to break the news. "Melody, I have something wonderful to tell you!"

I did my best to look curious.

"You're going to have a baby brother or sister real soon."

I grinned and did my best imitation of surprise and excitement. I reached out and hugged her. Then I patted her stomach and pointed to myself. She knew what I meant.

She looked me right in the eye. "We're gonna pray that this little one is fat and fine and healthy," she told me. "You know we love you, Melody — just as you are. But we're hoping this child doesn't have to face the challenges that you do."

Me too.

From then on, she put Dad in charge of lifting me. And although she never talked about it again in front of me, I knew she was worried. She gobbled gigantic green vitamin pills, ate lots of fresh oranges and apples, and she had this habit of touching her bulging belly and mumbling a prayer. I could tell that Dad was scared too, but his worry showed up in funny little ways, like bringing Mom piles of purple irises — her favorite flower — or fixing her gallons of grape Kool-Aid or big plates of grapes. I don't know what made Mom crave purple stuff.

Instead of watching hours and hours of the Discovery Channel, I found myself in my room staring at an empty TV screen — just thinking in the silence.

I knew that a new baby was really time-consuming. And I also knew *I* took up a lot of time. How would my parents ever have time for both of us?

Then a really horrible thought popped into my brain. What if they decided to look into Dr. Hugely's suggestions? I couldn't make the thought go away.

One Saturday afternoon a few months before the baby was born, I was curled up on our sofa, dozing. Mom had put pillows around me to make sure I didn't fall off. Butterscotch slept nearby, and Dad's favorite jazz station played a saxophone snoozer. Mom and Dad sat together on the smaller sofa, talking together quietly. I'm sure they thought I was asleep.

"What if?" Mom said, her voice tight.

"It won't be. The chances are *so* small, honey," Dad replied, but he sounded unsure.

"I couldn't *bear* it," Mom told him.

"You'd find the strength," he said calmly.

"But it's not going to happen. The odds are —"

"But what *if?*" she insisted, interrupting him, and for only the second time I could remember, my mother started to cry.

"Everything is gonna be fine," my father said, trying to soothe her. "We've got to think positive thoughts."

"It's all because of me," my mother said softly.

I perked up and listened harder.

"What do you mean?" Dad asked.

"It's my fault that Melody is like she is." Mom was crying really hard then. I could hardly make out her words.

"Diane, that's crazy! You can't hold on to that kind of guilt. These things just happen." I could tell Dad was trying to be reasonable.

"No! I'm the *mother!*" she wailed. "It was my *job* to bring a child into the world safely, and I screwed it up! Every other woman on the planet is able to give birth to a normal baby. There must be something wrong with *me!*"

"Sweetheart, it's not your fault. It's not your fault," and I could hear him pull my mom to him.

"But, Chuck, I'm so scared this baby is going to be messed up too!" she said in a shuddering breath.

"Please don't go there — don't even think like that," Dad murmured. "Statistically, what are the chances? Two children who . . ."

And I suddenly couldn't hear him anymore because my head was pulsing with the things I wanted to say but couldn't.

I wanted to tell Mom that I was sorry she was so sad and so scared.

That it wasn't her fault.

That I was just the way I was and she had nothing to do with it.

The part that hurt the most is I couldn't tell her any of it.

During Mom's entire pregnancy, however, my parents' attention to me never wavered, even though, yeah, I worried that it would. Dad did lots more as Mom got closer to her due date. He did some of the laundry, most of the cooking, and all the lifting and carrying. I got to school on time every day, got my stories read to me every night, and the three of us waited and hoped and prayed.

But Penny was born perfect and copper-bright, just like her name. From the minute she came home from the hospital, she was a really happy baby. Mom truly did carry a little bundle of joy into the house.

But I guess a new baby is rough on any parents, especially if they already have a kid like me at home. Sometimes there would be arguments. I could hear them through the bedroom wall.

"I need more help around here, Chuck," Mom would say, trying to keep her voice low.

"Well, you pay more attention to the baby than you do to me!"

"If you'd help more, I'd have more time for you! With two kids, and one of them Melody, it's not easy!"

"I have to go to work, you know!"

"I have a job too! Don't throw that in my face. Plus, I'm up twice a night to nurse the baby!"

"I know. I know. I'm sorry, Diane." Dad always softened and let Mom win.

"It's just I'm so tired all the time," Mom would say, her voice muffled.

"I'm sorry. I'll do better. I promise. I'll take off work tomorrow and take care of both girls. Why don't you go catch a movie or take Mrs. Valencia out to lunch?"

It would get quiet once more, but even so, somehow I always ended up feeling a teeny bit guilty. Life sure would be easier if they had only one child — one with working parts.

I once got one of those electronic dolls for Christmas. It was supposed to talk and cry and move its arms and legs if you pushed the right buttons. But when we opened the box, one of the arms had come off, and all the doll did, no matter which button you pushed, was squeak. Mom took it back to the store and got her money back.

I wonder if she ever wished she could get a refund for me.

But Penny! Penny really was a perfect baby. After just a few months she was sleeping through the night and smiling through each day. She sat up exactly when infants are supposed to, rolled over right on schedule, and crawled on cue. Amazing. And it seemed so easy! Sure, she fell on her face a few times, but once she got it, she was off.

Penny zoomed around like a little windup toy. She learned that the toilet was fun to splash in and that lamps will fall if you grab the cord. She learned that golden retrievers are not ponies, peas taste funny, dead flies on the floor are a no-no, but candy is really good. She laughed all the time. She learned her sister, Melody, couldn't do what she could do, but she didn't seem to care. So I tried not to care either.

Dad and his camcorder followed Penny around like the paparazzi follow a rock star!

We have hundreds of hours of footage of Penny being cute and doing adorable things. And, well, I admit it, sometimes I got kinda sick of watching a new video every time she learned something new. It sorta sucks to watch a baby do what you wish you could do.

Penny holding her own bottle.

Penny feeding herself teeny-tiny Cheerios from her high-chair tray.

Penny saying "ma-ma" and "da-da" just like the babies on *Sesame Street*.

Penny crawling on the floor and chasing Butterscotch.

Penny clapping her hands.

How did her little brain know how to tell her to pull herself up to a standing position? To hold on to the sofa for balance? How did she know how to stand on her own? Sometimes she'd fall over, but then she'd pop right back up. Never ever did she lie there, stuck like a turtle on its shell.

Dad still did our nighttime reading, but now it was Penny who snuggled on his lap. I was too big and too hard to balance, so I sat in my wheelchair, my dog at my feet, as the two of them read the stories I knew by heart. Butterscotch still slept only in my room. I liked that.

It really did make me glad to know Penny

was learning the same books I loved so much. I wondered if she was memorizing them. Probably not. She didn't need to.

I think Penny's third word was "Dee-Dee." She couldn't quite say "Melody," but she got the last part! I loved it when Mom put Penny in bed with me after her morning bath. She'd grab me and plant wet, baby-powder-smelling kisses all over my face. "Dee-Dee!" she'd say again and again.

By the time she was one year old, Penny could walk. She wobbled all over the house on her fat little legs. She fell a lot, dropping down on her butt, and laughing every time she did. Then she'd get back up and try it again.

That was something I'd never get to try.

With two kids in the house, our family routines changed. It took twice as long to get everybody ready each morning. Mom made sure Penny was dressed in pretty little outfits every day, even though she was just going next door to Mrs. V's house.

My clothes were okay, but I was noticing that lately they were more useful than cute. Mom seemed to be choosing them by how easy they'd be to get on me. It was kind of a bummer, but I knew I was getting heavier and heavier to lift, and so changing me was harder.

I probably should mention that feeding me is a real process. I can't chew very well, so I mostly get soft foods like scrambled eggs or oatmeal or applesauce. Since I can't hold a fork or spoon — I try, but I keep dropping them — someone has to place the food into my mouth, one spoonful at a time. It's slow.

Spoon, slurp, swallow.

Spoon, slurp, swallow.

Lots of food falls on the floor. Butterscotch likes that. She's like a canine vacuum cleaner.

Drinking stuff is hard for me too. I can't hold a glass and I can't sip from a straw, so somebody has to very carefully hold a cup to my lips and tip a little bit of liquid into my mouth so I can swallow. Too much and I choke and cough, and we have to start all over. It takes a long time to get a meal in me. I hate the whole process, obviously.

And some mornings were really stressful.

"Chuck! Can you bring me Melody's pink T-shirt from the clean clothes basket? She spilled juice all over her shirt!" Mom yelled up the stairs.

"Didn't you put a bib on her, Diane?" Dad yelled back. "You know she makes a mess! Why don't you wait and dress her *after* she eats?"

"So you want me to feed her naked? Just bring the shirt!" Mom snapped. "And a diaper for Penny. She's got a stinker."

"She's two — isn't she old enough to be potty trained?" Dad asked, coming downstairs with a blue T-shirt I had outgrown in one hand and a diaper in the other.

"Right. I'll get to potty training tonight — on the twenty-fifth hour of my day!"

Dad picked Penny up. "Uh-oh, that's a bad one," he said, his nose scrunched up. "Did you give her sweet potatoes again last night? I thought we stopped giving her those because they always give her the runs."

"Well, if *you* had gone to the grocery store like I asked, I could have given her something different! And that shirt is blue, not pink, and too small for Melody!"

Mom stormed out of the kitchen and up the stairs.

"Sorry, girls," Dad said to us. He whistled softly while he cleaned Penny up, threatening to call the Haz-mat team. That was funny.

Then he finished feeding me breakfast, not caring that my oatmeal was getting all over the juice-stained shirt. "Why not? May as well make a real mess and make it worth all the stress!" he said with a laugh.

I smiled at him and smeared oatmeal on

my tray.

Mom came back down with fresh makeup and a freshly painted-on smile, her hair done, and with my pink shirt. She and Dad hugged in the kitchen, both took a deep breath, and we actually made it out of the house on time.

We had lots of days like that.

CHAPTER 10

Penny wakes every morning asking for her "Doodle," a soft, brown stuffed animal that might be a monkey or maybe a squirrel. It's so beat-up, nobody knows for sure what it really is. She drags it everywhere. "Doodle!" she cries if it's been caught in her blankets. "Doodle!" she cries if it's right next to her. Of course, it sounds more like "doo-doo" when she says it. That makes Dad crack up.

I smile when I hear footsteps outside my door. Big ones and little tiny ones. My mom and Penny. And Doodle, of course. Sometimes my legs and arms are stiff from being in the same position all night, and sometimes my toes tingle. My bedroom door opens — Dad never gets around to fixing that squeak.

Mom traces a finger along my cheek. Maybe she's checking to see if I'm still breathing. I am. I open my eyes. I wish I could say, *Good morning,* but I just grin instead. She pulls me up and hugs me, rarely stopping to sit in the rocking chair anymore, and rushes me to the bathroom because I usually have to go really bad first thing in the morning.

Penny trails behind us, wearing a huge red and white hat like the one in *The Cat in the Hat* — the girl has a major hat obsession — and always with her Doodle. Butterscotch is never far from her. She lets Penny put hats on her and somehow endures Penny's hugs, which can sometimes feel more like choke holds. I've gotten a few! She barks to alert Mom or Dad if Penny gets too close to an electric plug or the front door.

Our bathroom is painted ocean blue and is large enough for Penny, Butterscotch, me and Mom — and my chair — without feeling crowded. That's a good thing, because we spend lots of time in there. Penny and I make pretty big messes. But at least I don't have to wear diapers. It's bad enough that someone has to put me on the toilet, but diapers? Yuck!

Even though the doctors said it would be impossible, by the time I was three, Mom had me potty trained like any other kid my age. I hated sitting in dirty diapers, and she hated changing them, so I figured out a way to let her know I had to go, and she'd hustle me to the toilet.

Mom and I can sometimes talk without words. I point to the ceiling, and she somehow just knows whether I'm talking about the ceiling fan, the moon, or the dark spot where the rain leaked through during the last thunderstorm. She can tell if I'm sad, and she can sense when I need a hug. She rubs my back and makes me relax when I'm tense and upset. She tells dirty jokes sometimes when Dad isn't listening, and we both crack up.

One morning, as she was getting me dressed for school, I pointed to her stomach, then covered my eyes as if the sight were too much to look at. It was shortly after Penny had been born, and she still had a good-size baby bulge.

"You calling me fat?" she asked, acting insulted.

I laughed a little and said, "uh," which is the closest thing I've got to a *yes.*

"Take it back!" she said, tickling the bottom of my feet.

Instead, I held my arms out like I was making a big circle and laughed out loud. *Huge! Enormous! Like an elephant!* I could tell she knew what I was thinking.

We both rolled with laughter, and then she hugged me tight. I wish I could tell her

I loved her.

Mom knows when I'm hungry or thirsty, and whether I need a glass of milk or just some water. She can tell if I'm really sick or simply faking it, because sometimes I do pretend I don't feel good just so I can stay home. She can tell what my temperature is just by feeling my forehead. She only uses the thermometer to prove she's right.

I can tell stuff about what she is thinking too. By the end of the day, after she's been at the hospital all day, then fixed dinner, then bathed Penny and me and put me in bed, I can tell she's kinda reached her max. She breathes hard. Her forehead is sweating. I sometimes reach out and touch her hand with mine. I can feel her calm down, and she'll trace her fingers along my cheek, just like she does in the morning, and give me a kiss good night.

Every Saturday morning after I've been fed, Mom reads the newspaper while she has her coffee and Penny smashes bananas on her high-chair tray. Butterscotch doesn't like fruit, but she stays close by, just in case somebody drops a piece of bacon. Mom's off on weekends, so she relaxes. She sometimes reads articles to me or tells me about the latest hurricane or uprising or explosion in the world.

"More fighting in the Middle East," she says.

I've seen it on TV. Bombs and tears and faces of fear.

"There's a new Superman movie coming out soon," she reads as she shakes the newspaper flat. "Maybe we can go catch a matinee."

I love superheroes. I guess Superman is my favorite because he can fly. How great would *that* be?

Mom reads me the comic pages also. I like Garfield.

"Garfield is cheating on his diet again," Mom says. "He ate Jon's lasagna and Odie's meatballs."

I laugh and point at Mom's hips.

"You calling me fat again, Miss Dee-Dee? Just because I finished off your spaghetti last night?"

I grin.

"You'll be sorry when I start feeding everybody lettuce for lunch!"

We both laugh. Mom's not even close to being fat, but I like to tease her.

For my tenth birthday I got a whole book of Garfield cartoons — now, that's what's up! I made Dad read it to me over and over. Garfield is a cat who has a lot to say, but all his words are written in little circles above his head. He can't really talk, of course — he's a cat!

But sometimes that's how I feel — like wouldn't it be cool if I had somebody to write the words over my head so people would know what I'm thinking? I could live with that — large floating bubbles above me, speaking for me.

Wouldn't it be cool if somebody could invent a bubble-talking machine before fifth grade starts in a couple of weeks? Hah!

When I try to talk, the words are exploding in my brain, but all that comes out are meaningless sounds and squeaks. Penny can say lots of words and pieces of words. But my lips won't come together to make even simple sounds like that, so most of my noises are vowels. I can say "uh" and "ah" pretty clearly, and, if I concentrate, sometimes I can squeeze out a "buh" or a "huh." But that's it.

My parents can usually figure out what I need just by listening carefully. To outsiders, I probably sound like one of those children who was raised by wolves. My communication board, even with everything Mrs. V has added to it — well, it sorta sucks.

For example, one afternoon earlier this summer, I had a taste for a Big Mac and a shake. Vanilla. I love fast food. Mom wasn't home, and getting my father to figure out what I want is sometimes a big job. I pointed to the picture of my dad, the word **go**, the word **eat**, and a happy face. That's all I had to work with. I gotta give him credit — he tried. He asked me a million questions, so I could point to **yes** or **no**.

"Are you hungry?"

Yes.

"Okay, I'll fix you some tuna salad."

No. I pounded on the tray.

"I thought you said you were hungry. Do you want some spaghetti?"

No. Gentler this time.

"So what do you want?"

No answer. Nothing on my board could describe it. I pointed to **go** again.

"You want me to go in the kitchen and cook you something?"

No.

"You want me to go to the grocery store?"

No. I was starting to get upset, pounding the board with my right thumb once more.

"I don't get it. You said you wanted me to get you something to eat."

Yes. Once again I pointed to Dad's picture, then **go**, then **eat**, then happy face.

I could feel one of my tornado explosions starting. I started to kick, and my arms got all tight. It was driving me *crazy* that I

100

couldn't tell him about a stupid Big Mac.

"Calm down, sweetheart," Dad said softly.

My jaws felt like steel bars. I knew I was breathing hard, and my tongue wouldn't stay in my mouth. I hit my board once more, aiming at no word in particular.

"Argwk!" I screeched.

"I'm sorry, Melody, but I can't figure out what you mean. I'm going to fix you some noodles and cheese. Will that be okay?"

I sighed, gave up, and pointed to **yes**. I calmed down while he cooked. The noodles were pretty good.

A couple of weeks later my dad and I were in the car and we passed by a McDonald's. I screeched and kicked and pointed like Godzilla was coming down the street. Dad must have thought I was nuts. Finally, he said, "Would you like to stop and get a Big Mac and a shake for dinner tonight as a treat?"

I shouted, "Uh!" as loud as I could, and kept on kicking with absolute delight as he pulled into the drive-through. He never did make the connection between that fast-food stop and my request a couple of weeks earlier. But that's okay. Even though it took us an hour to finish, it was one of the best hamburgers I've ever had.

CHAPTER 11

Fifth grade started a few weeks ago, and a couple of cool things have happened. Well, I didn't get a gadget that makes Garfield-like speech bubbles over my head, but I did get an electric wheelchair, and our school began something called "inclusion classes." I thought that was funny. I've never been included in anything. But these classes are supposed to give kids like me a chance to interact with what everybody else calls the "normal" students. What's normal? Duh!

Comparing my new chair to my old one is like comparing a Mercedes to a skateboard. The wheels are almost like car tires, which makes the ride smooth and easy, like riding on pillows. I can't go very fast, but I can propel myself down the hall with just a little lever on the handrail. Or, if I flip the switch to manual, I can still be pushed if necessary.

When Freddy first saw it, he shouted,

"Woo-hoo!" like I'd just won the Indy 500. "Melly go zoom zoom now! Wanna race?" He spun his own chair in excited circles around me.

I'm sure he could beat me, even at the subatomic speeds our chairs are set to.

My electric chair is a lot heavier than my manual chair, and it's almost impossible for Mom and Dad to lift anywhere. "When you decide to switch to a rocket ship for transportation," Dad joked at first, rubbing his back, "you're gonna need to hire Superman to get it in the car!"

I grinned. But I know he saw the thanks in my eyes.

So he bought a set of portable wheelchair ramps that fold and fit in the back of our SUV. With those, he can roll the new chair into the back of our car and still have back muscles left over.

For me, it's all about the freedom. Now I don't have to wait for somebody to move me across the room. I can just go there. Nice. So when they decided to start mainstreaming us into the regular classes, the electric chair was really helpful.

Our fifth-grade teacher in room H-5 reminds me of a television grandmother. Mrs. Shannon is pudgy, wears lavender body lotion every single day, and I think she must be from the South because she talks with a real strong drawl. Somehow it makes everything she says seem more interesting.

She told us on the first day, "I'm gonna bust a gut makin' sure y'all get all you can out of this school year, you hear? We're gonna read, and learn, and grow. I believe every one of y'all got potential all stuffed inside, and together we're gonna try to make some of that stuff shine."

I liked her. She brought in stacks of new books to read to us, as well as games and music and videos. Unlike Mrs. Billups, Mrs. Shannon must have read all our records because she dusted off the headphones and even brought in more books on tape for me.

"Ya'll ready for music class?" she asked us one morning. "Let's get this inclusion stuff goin'!"

I jerked with excitement. As the aides helped us down the hall to the music room, I wondered if I'd get to sit next to a regular kid. What if I did something stupid? What if Willy yodeled, or Carl farted? Maria was likely to blurt out something crazy. Would this be our only chance? What if we messed this up? I could barely contain myself. We were going to be in a *regular* classroom!

The music teacher, Mrs. Lovelace, had been the first to volunteer to open her class to us. The music room was huge — almost twice as large as our classroom. My hands got sweaty.

The kids in there were mostly fifth graders too. They'd probably be surprised to know that I knew all their names. I've watched them on the playground at lunch and at recess for years. My classmates sit under a tree and catch a breeze while they play kickball or tag, so I know who they are and how they work. I doubted if they knew any of *us* by name, though.

Well, the whole thing was almost a disaster. Willy, probably upset and scared about being in a new room, started yelping at the top of his lungs. Jill began to cry. She held tightly to the hand grips of her walker and refused to move past the doorway. I wanted to disappear.

All of the "normal" children in the music class — I guess about thirty of them — turned to stare. Some of them laughed. Others looked away. But one girl in the back row crossed her arms across her chest and scowled at her classmates who were acting up.

Two girls, Molly and Claire — everyone knew them because they were mean to almost everybody on the playground — mimicked Willy. They made sure they stayed just out of the teacher's line of sight. But I saw it. So did Willy.

"Hey, Claire!" Molly said, twisting her arms above her head and bending her body so it looked crooked. "Look at me! I'm a retard!" She laughed so hard, she snorted snot.

Claire cracked up as well, then let spit dribble out of her mouth. "Duh buh wuh buh," she said, crossing her eyes and pretending to slip out of her chair.

Mrs. Lovelace finally noticed them, because she said sternly, "Stand up please, Claire."

"I didn't do anything!" Claire replied.

"You stand as well, Molly," Mrs. Lovelace added.

"We were just laughing," Molly said defensively. But she stood up next to Claire.

Mrs. Lovelace took both girls' chairs and slid them over to the wall.

"Why'd you do that?" Claire cried out in protest.

"You have perfectly good bodies and legs that work. Use them," Mrs. Lovelace instructed.

"You can't make us stand the whole class!" Claire moaned.

"The board of education requires that I teach you music. There is nothing in the rule book that requires you sit down while I do it. Now stand there and be quiet, or I'll send you to the office for showing disrespect to our guests."

They stood. In the middle of the third row of chairs, where everyone else was seated comfortably, they stood.

This teacher is awesome!

After that, things went more smoothly. Jill, who had continued to cry, had been taken back to our room by one of the aides. The rest of us sat quietly in the back of the room.

Mrs. Lovelace began class once more. "I think we need a moment to gather ourselves, children." She sat down at her piano and began to play "Moon River," and then she switched to the theme song from one of those new vampire movies. Oh, yeah, she knew what we liked. When I started seeing the colors, I knew she was good. Forest green, lime green, emerald.

I glanced over at Gloria. Instead of sitting all curled up like she usually did, her arms were outstretched like she was trying to catch the music and bring it to her. Her face was almost glowing. She began to sway with the music.

Then Mrs. Lovelace completely changed tempo and played the opening notes to "Take Me Out to the Ball Game." Willy clapped his hands wildly.

Finally, the teacher started to play "Boogie Woogie Bugle Boy." Dad would have loved it. Kids started to shimmy in their seats. Maria got up and started dancing! She clapped loudly, never quite on the beat, but to a rhythm that was all her own.

Mrs. Lovelace paused at the end of the song. "Music is powerful, my young friends," she said. "It can connect us to memories. It can influence our mood and our responses to problems we might face."

She cut her eyes at Claire and Molly, who still stood in the empty places where their chairs had been.

I wanted to tell Mrs. Lovelace I liked music too. I wanted to know if she'd ever heard the song "Elvira" or if she would teach us how to make our own music. I tried to raise my hand, but she didn't notice me. It must have looked like just another one of those random movements that kids like me seem to make. But I had the feeling that Mrs. Lovelace was someone who'd take the time to figure me out.

The teacher went on. "Before I continue with the lesson, let's make this a real inclusion experience. Perhaps our friends from room H-5 would like to sit with the rest of us instead of being stuck in the back."

Freddy heard that and took his chance. He put his chair into gear and zoomed to the front of that big room and shouted, "I am Freddy. I like music. I go fast!"

The class laughed. I can tell the difference between people making fun of us and people being nice to us. Freddy could too, so he joined in the laughter. Mrs. Lovelace looked momentarily startled, then went over to Freddy, shook his hand, and welcomed him to the class. She sat him right there in front, next to a boy named Rodney. Rodney gave Freddy a high five, and the two of them grinned at each other. Okay, I had to admit it — I was jealous.

Mrs. Lovelace asked an aide to bring Gloria down front close to the piano. A girl named Elizabeth glanced at Gloria nervously, but she didn't move away when Gloria was wheeled next to her.

Elizabeth's best friend is a girl named Jessica. At recess they sit together near the fence and share granola bars. I've always wondered what they whisper about. I also noticed that everything Elizabeth does, Jessica tries to outdo. Like, if Elizabeth beats her running to the fence, Jessica insists they run again so she can win too. Or if Elizabeth gets a new book bag, Jessica will have a new one the next day.

So when Elizabeth started talking to Gloria, who looked terrified, Jessica raised her hand and asked if one of the H-5 kids could sit next to her.

Maria might have trouble figuring out some stuff, but she's a real friendly person. "I wanna sit by the blue-shirt girl. I wanna sit by the blue-shirt girl," she demanded. She stomped down to Jessica's seat and sat down next to her. Then she jumped back up and gave Jessica a hug, then gave a hug to the kids sitting closest to Jessica. One kid stiffened up when she touched him, but I was surprised that most of them let her hug them. Molly and Claire, since they were standing, had no choice.

"Ooh, yuck!" Claire whispered.

"Cooties!" Molly whispered back.

Mrs. Lovelace raised an eyebrow, then cleared her throat. "It seems you two like to stand. You'll continue to do so the rest of this week."

"Aw, man! This sucks!" I heard Claire say.

Molly had sense enough to say nothing.

Maria didn't notice. She even kissed Claire on the cheek. That was funny.

Willy ended up next to a large, friendly boy named Connor.

Ashley and Carl were absent that day, so that left me sitting in the back of the classroom by myself. The room got real quiet. I suddenly felt cold, like the air-conditioning had been cranked up real high. I got goose bumps.

The teacher looked around the room, expectation on her face, I guess hoping that somebody would volunteer to take me. At that moment I would have given anything to be back in our bluebird room instead of sitting there with thirty kids staring at me.

Finally, a girl got up out of her seat and walked over to my chair. She squatted down and looked me directly in the face. Then she smiled. It was the girl with the long hair who had frowned at her friends for laughing. "I'm Rose," she said, her voice soft.

I smiled back, and I tried really hard not to kick or grunt or make a noise that would scare her away. I held my breath and thought about calm, quiet things, like ocean waves. It worked. I inhaled deeply and slowly, then pointed on my board to **Thank you**. Rose seemed to understand.

I showed her I could power my own chair, and I rolled to where she'd been sitting. We sat together for the rest of that class. And I didn't do a single embarrassing thing! It ended way too soon.

But ever since, every Wednesday, our little class of outcasts gets to join Mrs. Lovelace's music class. It's awesome!

Jill, Ashley, and Carl eventually became a part of the group. Each one of us has been assigned a "buddy" to sit next to and interact with.

Once they met her, all the girls rushed to be Ashley's buddy. I think it's like playing with a pretty little doll for them, but Ashley seems to like the attention.

Claire and Molly eventually got their chairs returned, but they haven't chosen to be buddies for anybody yet. That's fine with me.

Elizabeth and Jessica have stuck with Gloria and Maria. Jill sits contentedly next to a girl named Aster Cheng. Rodney actually comes over at recess and talks to Freddy. Sometimes he pushes Freddy really fast in his chair. Freddy loves that.

And I get to sit with Rose every single Wednesday. On Tuesday, I can hardly sleep because I'm so excited. I make my mother pick out my nicest clothes on Wednesday morning — cool outfits like the other kids wear. I screech at her until she gets just the right combination. I make sure she brushes my teeth so my breath won't stink.

I think about Rose all the time. I worry that she will change her mind and not like me. But Rose talks to me like I understand,

and she tries to figure out what I'm saying as well. One day I pointed to **new** and **shoes** and **nice** on my communication board, then down to her feet, to let her know that I had noticed she got new sneakers and that I liked them. At first she seemed surprised that I could do this. Especially since it sometimes takes me a long time to make my thoughts make sense using my board. One day I pointed to **music** and **bad** and **stinky**, then I started laughing. Rose didn't get it at first. So I pointed to the words again, then pointed to Mrs. Lovelace, who was playing some kind of jazz music on the CD player. I'm like Mom — not a big jazz fan; it confuses me because it doesn't have a tune.

Rose finally figured it out and said, "Oh! You don't like jazz? Me neither!" We both laughed so hard, Mrs. Lovelace had to put her finger to her lips to tell us to hush. Never in my life have I had a teacher tell me to be quiet because I was talking to somebody in class! It was the best feeling in the world! I felt like the rest of the kids.

Rose tells me secrets sometimes. I know she bites her fingernails, and she hates milk. She goes to church every Sunday but falls asleep until it's over. Me too. She has a younger sister just like I do. She even likes country music. Sometimes she tells me about trips to the mall with her friends. It would be so tight to be able to do that.

CHAPTER 12

By the end of October the inclusion program has been expanded. Maria and Jill have been added to art and gym classes, and Freddy and Willy go to science. Me — it's the first time I've ever gotten to change classes for different subjects in my life!

Now when the bell rings, instead of wondering what's happening out there in the halls, I'm out there too. It's awesome. I plow through the crowds in my electric chair like a power mower in thick grass.

Sometimes kids wave or say, "What's up?" Every once in a while someone will even walk with me to the next class. Cool.

But "inclusion" doesn't mean I'm included in *everything.* I usually sit in the back of the room, going crazy because I know answers to things and can't tell anybody.

"What's the definition of the word 'dignity'?" one of my teachers asked a few days ago. Of course I knew, so I raised my hand, but the teacher didn't notice the small movement I'm able to make. And even if she were to call on me, what then? I can't very well yell out the answers. It's really frustrating.

During parent conferences earlier this month, my parents came in to meet Mrs. Shannon and the other teachers. Instead of leaving me on my own in a corner somewhere, Mrs. Shannon pulled me into the circle of teachers who are involved in the inclusion program. She is so great!

She patted the arm of my chair and smiled. "This child's got some serious smarts! She's going to be our star in this program."

I did my usual screeching and kicking. I think I would have kissed her if I could, but that would have been pretty sloppy, I guess.

"Well, it's about time somebody recognizes what we've always known," my dad told Mrs. Shannon. "We really appreciate the opportunity to let her show what she can do."

Mom was especially pleased to find out I'd been assigned a "mobility assistant" — an aide of my own.

"Finally!" Mom said, relief in her voice. "We've been asking for this for years."

"Budget-bustin' paperwork. A system that

runs on grits instead of good sense. I'm so sorry," Mrs. Shannon replied, shaking her head. "I'm trying to get all the students in H-5 the services they need. But I smacked an aide for Melody way up on top of my list, so we'll see how it goes. I'm expecting a wonderful school year!"

So cool, I tapped on my board.

An aide! Wow. This person's job would be to take me to classes, sit with me, and help me participate. I wondered what she'd look like. Or maybe I'd get a guy. Would he be young and cute, or old and grumpy?

The very next day my new aide was at school before I was, chatting with Mrs. Shannon in room H-5 as we kids were wheeled in. She came right over to me and took my hand. "Hi, Melody. I'm glad to meet you. My name is Catherine. I go to the university, and I'm gonna be your deals and wheels every day."

She talked to me like I was just like any other student, not a kid in a wheelchair. I tried not to kick, but it was hard to hold in my excitement.

"Cute T-shirt," she said as she checked out Tweety Bird on the front of the new lavender top Mom had bought for me.

I pointed to **thanks** on my board.

"What's your favorite color?" she asked then.

I pointed to **purple**, but then quickly slid my thumb over to **green**. I grinned at her.

"You're quick, Melody. I can see we both like weird colors. We're going to get along just fine." Catherine was dressed in purple tennis shoes, green tights, a purple suede skirt, and the ugliest green sweater I've ever seen.

I wanted to tease her about her outfit, but I didn't want her to think I was mean. After all, I'd just met her. I searched all over my board for a way to jokingly make fun of her clothes, but I couldn't think of a way to do it. So I gave up. It is *so* hard to say stuff.

So now it's Catherine who helps me at lunch so I don't make a mess. And Catherine who reads off the answers I point to on my board. She's added some more words and phrases to it. And she helped Mrs. Shannon order the books I need to read. She even makes sure the headphones don't fall off my ears.

The "regular" fifth-grade language arts teacher, Miss Gordon, is not much older than Catherine. She almost explodes with energy and makes books seem like live-action plays. She jumps up on the table. Sometimes she sings. She lets the class act out parts of stories, and sometimes she even turns books into games.

"Vocabulary bingo!" Miss Gordon announced one morning. "Doughnuts to the winning team!"

As they played, my classmates broke their necks to get the right definition, screamed out answers, and groaned when they messed up. In just half an hour every student in the room knew all twenty vocabulary words. Miss Gordon gave doughnuts to the losing team, too, but the winners got the ones with the chocolate sprinkles.

I knew all of the definitions, but the other kids moved too fast for me. Chocolate would have made a mess of my clothes anyway.

One unusually warm day this week, Miss Gordon brought in fans and spray bottles of water and let us eat Popsicles in class. Orange ones, of course, in honor of Halloween, while she read poems about pumpkins and ghosts. Catherine held my Popsicle for me with a paper towel under my chin. We didn't spill one drop!

Miss Gordon does other cool things too. Like when she decided the class would read the story of Anne Frank, she had kids take turns squeezing into a small space she had built under a table so they could understand how Anne might have felt. I couldn't do that, but I got the idea.

And she's assigned other great books this semester. I'm reading — well, listening to — *Shiloh* by Phyllis Reynolds Naylor and *The Giver* by Lois Lowry. And there's one called *Tuck Everlasting* — the kid never gets to grow up. Staying a child forever is not as cool as folks may think.

Because of Mrs. V, I could actually read the books. But the print is usually very small, and it's hard for my eyes to stay on the right line. And nobody has figured out the best way for me to hold on to a book without it falling on the floor a million times, so I usually choose the audiobook instead of the written version.

I even take tests now! Catherine reads me the questions, and I point to the answers on the sheets she places on my tray. I pass every single test, and she doesn't help me one single bit. I would probably get 100 percent on each one, but some of the questions require long answers I just can't explain with the words on my board.

One time, in spelling, Miss Gordon read the words aloud, and I pointed to the letters on my board. Catherine wrote down what I pointed to so I could follow along with the test. Claire and Molly, who are always watching me, it feels like, began to complain.

"It's not fair!" Claire cried, waving her hand to get Miss Gordon's attention.

"Catherine cheats for her!" Molly added.

What *is* it with those two? It's like they're jealous of me or something. And that's just plain crazy.

At the same time, I realized that they actually thought I had it easier! That sure was a first.

Last Monday morning Miss Gordon told the class, "As some of you may know, because I do this every year, our long-range fifth-grade project this year is our biography unit. We will read the biographies of famous people, do a report on a famous person of your choosing, and each of you will also write your own autobiography."

"Well, it's gotta be short. What can you do in eleven years?" Connor, the big kid, shouted out. Everybody laughed.

"In your case, Connor," Miss Gordon replied, "I'm sure you'll think of way too much."

"Can I do my report on the guy who invented hamburgers?" Connor asked to more laughter.

"I doubt if we know who made the first burger, but you *can* do your report on the person who founded McDonald's. He got rich off hamburgers and fries."

"Awesome. My kind of dude," Connor said.

Rose raised her hand. I love the fact that she's in all my inclusion classes. "Miss Gordon, when is all this due?"

Rose is the type of student who takes all kinds of notes in a bright red spiral planner and never misses a homework assignment.

"Relax, Rose. We've got until the end of May, and I'll walk you through each segment, one step at a time. Tomorrow we'll talk about how to write your memories."

Rose seemed satisfied, but I noticed she scribbled almost a whole page in her notebook. I'd give anything to do that. But working on stuff the teachers in the regular classes assign is just plain awesome.

History class is even better than language arts class, even though the teacher, a man named Mr. Dimming, has none of Miss Gordon's spark. Balding and pudgy, he's been teaching at the school for over twenty years, and kids say he's never been absent — not even once. Clearly, he loves what he does. His car is always in the parking lot when our bus rolls in and always there when we leave for the day. He dresses like a TV preacher — in three-piece suits with vests most days. I've never seen him without a crisp white shirt and a colorful tie. I wonder if his wife picks them out — some of them are really sharp.

Mr. D loves history. He can quote facts and dates and wars and generals like somebody on a game show. I bet he could win on *Jeopardy.*

The other students don't seem to like Mr. Dimming much. They call him "Dimwit Dimming" behind his back. I think that's sorta mean because Mr. D is really smart — smart enough to run the quiz team.

When Mr. Dimming got to American presidents in class, I rocked! He gave the students a list of presidents and all their vice presidents and told us there would be a test in a week. Catherine read the names to me several times.

"I've never even heard of some of these men," she admitted to me as we went over the list the first time. "Hannibal Hamlin was Abraham Lincoln's first vice president. Who knew?"

I memorized them all.

When Mr. Dimming gave the test, all I had to do was point to the right answers. He checked to make sure that Catherine wasn't helping me. I even finished before some of the others.

While Mr. D was returning the test papers, he gave the class a few minutes of free time to sharpen pencils or stretch or talk. I was surprised to see Rose walking toward my desk.

"How did you do on the test, Melody?" she asked. "I only got a seventy-five." She looked disappointed.

I'd gotten an eighty-five, but I was so excited that she'd come over to me that I got all mixed up. So I pointed to 5 and then 8 on my board.

She touched my arm, her eyes full of sympathy. "Don't worry," she said. "You'll do better next time."

And she did this right in front of Molly and Claire and the rest of the class. There was no way I was going to tell her what I really got on the test.

I tried to think of something to say so she'd stay longer. **Pretty** and **shirt** was all I could come up with using my lame board. I sure could use a word choice that said *Cool outfit,* but somehow Mrs. V had overlooked that one.

But Rose beamed. "You look nice today too!"

I really didn't. I had on a faded blue sweatshirt and matching sweatpants. Mom hardly got me anything else these days. But

I *hate* sweat suits. If I could choose, I'd wear blue jeans with sparkly decals, a blouse with decorated buttons, and a vest!

But I had no way to tell Rose that, so I just pointed to **thank you**. Incredibly, she touched my arm one more time, then she went back to her seat and her friends.

Then the bell rang, class was over, and I had to go back to H-5. No more inclusion, no more Rose. And four more hours of school left. Even Catherine left. She had afternoon classes at the university and hurried to get there on time.

Mrs. Shannon was out sick that day, so I sat quietly with Ashley and Maria and Carl and Willy while we watched *The Lion King* — again. I've seen it a million times — I can quote it. Then the substitute teacher gave us a math lesson. Addition — again. When am I ever gonna get to long division?

I wondered what Rose was doing. It was a very long afternoon.

CHAPTER 13

"Penny! Nooooo!" Mrs. V calls out.

Dragging Doodle behind her, Penny has scooted out of Mrs. V's front door and is halfway down the ramp from her porch, shouting, "Bye-bye!" from under her green baseball cap. Butterscotch, at home in our backyard, would be having a doggie fit if she could see Penny trying to bolt.

It's one of those early November days that an artist would love. Red-bronze leaves. Bright gold sunlight. Leftover summer. I don't blame Penny for trying to bolt.

Mrs. V scoops her up and brings her back in the house.

"Goin' work." Penny pouts.

"Not today, honey buns," Mrs. V says firmly as she locks the front door.

Penny loves wearing hats and playing dress-up. Mom rarely buys fancy church-lady hats for herself, but for Penny, she'll sometimes pick out a crazy-looking straw

126

hat with bows and ribbons and bring it home.

At home Penny spends a crazy amount of time in front of the hall mirror with a couple of Mom's plastic necklaces hanging down almost to her shoes, a purse on each arm, and a hat tilted sideways on her head. "Gotta go work," she'll say, with one hand on her hip.

"Who has she ever seen dressed like that going to work?" Mom asks as we all crack up.

"She's only two! I'm not going to be able to afford the kid when she's old enough to go shopping on her own," Dad always says. He snaps every cute pose she makes with his cell phone camera.

When Mrs. V sets Penny back down, Penny pokes her lips out, throws Doodle on the floor, and wraps both her arms around her chest. I laugh. I wish I had enough co-ordination to have "attitude"!

"Here, Penny, why don't you just sit down and draw me a picture instead," Mrs. V says, whipping out a box of crayons.

Attitude forgotten, Penny grabs a handful and promptly begins to scribble all over the coloring book, as well as Mrs. V's table.

I wish I could use crayons. I'd draw a rose, with a velvety red bloom and a green stem

127

and yellow-green leaves coming from it. I can see it so clearly in my mind, but, of course, when I put a pencil or crayon in my stupid-tight little fingers, all I can manage are squiggly lines. Nothing that looks even close to a rose.

I want to draw it for Rose. She has rose designs on her notebooks and book bag. I don't know where her mother finds such cool stuff. Rose's name really fits her — she's pretty and delicate and nice to be around. If she has thorns like real roses do, I've never noticed.

While Penny is busy with her crayons, Mrs. V checks her mail. She opens several envelopes, then gasps with surprise. "Guess what, girls?" she exclaims. "I've won a contest!"

I look at her with interest. Penny continues to scribble, ignoring both of us.

"I entered an essay contest at the bookstore in the mall," she explains to me. "The topic was why fish are important in our world ecology."

I point to **food** on my board and smirk.

"No, silly." She reaches over and tickles me. "I wrote something about oceans and the balance of nature — I don't honestly remember what I said — but I won first prize: a trip for six to the new downtown aquarium. All expenses paid. Stupendous!"

I've seen the commercials on television for the aquarium — it's supposed to have sharks and turtles and penguins and a million other sea animals. **Go?** I ask by pointing on my board.

"Well, besides me, I don't know who else to take," she says, scratching her head and grinning.

I kick my foot straps loose. *Me! Me!* I want to scream. Instead, I point to myself.

"Hmmm. Who could I take?" Mrs. V teases, looking around the kitchen. I can tell she's trying hard not to laugh.

Me! Me! I jab.

"Well, of course I'll take you, Mello Yello," Mrs. V says, smiling. "Just think of all the new words we'll gather. I'm going to write down the names of every single fish for you to learn!"

I slap my head, pretending to be upset.

"So, if I take you and Penny, your mom and dad, and me, that's five. I wonder who else we could take?" She scrunches up her face, thinking.

I know immediately. Rose could go with us! I spell out her name. **R-O-S-E**. And again. **R-O-S-E**. Then I hit **Please**.

"Hmmm. Your friend Rose from school?" I buck and kick with excitement. "I think that's a great idea, Melody. I'll ask your parents and her parents, and if she's willing, we'll have a wonderful day."

I can't stop kicking my feet!

It takes several weeks before both Mom and Dad are off work on a Saturday, but Thanksgiving weekend ends up working out for everybody. I have trouble sleeping the night before. Rose's parents seem really nice from what I could tell from listening to Mom's end of the conversation. I couldn't believe Rose wanted to come! She wanted to come with me, the kid in the chair!

At school Rose whispered with me about the trip, just like I'd seen other kids do when they have secrets. I felt like a real girl.

Now that the Saturday is finally here, we all pile into our SUV early in the morning. Even though the weather has turned pretty chilly, I made sure Mom put a really nice outfit on me — cute jeans and no sweats. Rose hasn't said anything about what I'm wearing, but she keeps cooing over Penny.

"Your sister is adorable, Melody!" Rose says. I smile and nod.

Penny reaches out her chubby little hands and claps. "Wo-sie," she says.

"I think she said my name!" Rose exclaims. "Your sister is not only cute, she's a genius!"

As we drive, Rose chatters with my parents and Mrs. V like she's known them all her life. I watch it all silently, thinking this has to be the best day of my life.

When we get to the aquarium, Dad unloads my chair and eases me into it while Mom gets Penny's stroller out and straps her in. Rose pushes Penny as Mom pushes me, so we can be side by side.

The place is crowded — I guess because it's a holiday weekend. Nobody pays any attention to me, which is perfect. I can almost forget who I am.

Inside, fish tanks go from floor to ceiling. I think of Ollie. He might have been happy here. In one tank sharks swim overhead, just like we're actually looking up from the ocean floor. Okay, so Ollie might not have been so happy in *that* tank.

I've never seen so many fish — from all over the world, it seems. Fish with spikes and spots. Fish with markings so beautiful, they look painted.

Penny slaps at the glass whenever a fish comes close. "Fishies! More fishies!" Mrs. V, as promised, writes down names of species and takes pictures so I can remember when we get back home. Mom and Dad whisper together like teenagers. I've never seen them so relaxed.

We stop in front of every tank. I love the jellyfish, which remind me of streams of shiny cloth, and the lion-fish, which really do look a little like swimming lions. At the sea horse tank Rose observes that their heads point backward! She seems to be having a great time.

Then, from around the corner, come the two people I'd least want to run into: Molly and Claire. They are with a Girl Scout troop. They're fake bumping into each other, not paying much attention to their group leader, who is telling them about the percentage of salt found in ocean water.

Molly and Claire, dressed exactly alike in jeans, long-sleeved T-shirts, and Scout vests, look at Rose with surprise.

"Hey, Rose! You here with your mom?" Claire asks.

"Uh, no," Rose says evasively, walking away from us and toward them.

"Your dad?" Molly says, looking at me like I smell bad. And she's acting like my parents are invisible.

"I'm here with Melody and her family," Rose mumbles.

"On purpose?" Claire shrieks. Both she and Molly start laughing loudly.

"It's not so bad," Rose says quietly. But I heard her.

Mom starts to say something to the girls, but Dad takes her arm. "They're children," he tells her. "Let them work it out themselves."

Mom has those daggers in her eyes — the sharp points she shoots at people who say dumb things about me — but she stays quiet. Her fists are balled.

Mrs. V, however, isn't going to let anybody stop her. From her almost-six-foot height, she towers over Molly and Claire. "You! Girl with braces on her teeth!" Claire looks up at her, stunned.

"Yes, ma'am?" Claire has sense enough to say.

"Why do you think your parents spent good money getting you braces?"

"Huh?" Claire looks confused. Molly has quietly disappeared into her Scout troop.

"Your teeth were imperfect, so your parents got you braces. One day you'll thank them when you get a date for the prom," Mrs. V roars. The whole Scout troop, plus a few other visitors to the aquarium, stop to listen to her.

"What do my teeth have to do with anything?" Claire asks, looking around nervously.

"Some people get braces on their teeth. Some get braces on their legs. For others, braces won't work, so they need wheelchairs and walkers and such. You're a lucky girl that you only had messed-up teeth. Remember that."

"Yes, ma'am," Claire says again. Then she scurries off to join her friends.

Rose walks back to us then, a little embarrassed, I think. "Claire can be clueless," she whispers to me.

You think?

After a few more tanks Penny gets tired and starts to whine, so we leave the aquarium before we even get to see the penguins. We take Rose home and she thanks us properly and says she had a real good time.

But did she?

CHAPTER 14

The Monday following Thanksgiving break, Catherine and I roll into Miss Gordon's language arts class a few minutes before the bell. It doesn't look like I'll ever find out what Rose really thought about the trip to the aquarium because she clearly has more exciting things on her mind.

Everyone is huddled around her desk.

"Awesome!"

"I love the color — I didn't know they come in lime green!"

"Oh, man, that's what's up!"

"How many songs have you downloaded so far?"

"What's your new e-mail address?"

"You got IM?"

"Videos! That's so tight!"

"I wish my mom would get me a laptop like that."

I roll closer. Rose is showing off a brand-new laptop computer.

"I can get on the Internet and find stuff for school and type up all my homework," she's telling the group around her. "I've already uploaded pictures of my dog, and I've got my own MySpace page!"

I just shake my head as Catherine takes me back to my usual place in the back of the room. A laptop. I'm still pointing to words and phrases that Mrs. V and my mother have taped to a board that's strapped to my wheelchair, and Rose has the Internet — I guess that means the whole universe — at her fingertips.

I close my eyes, trying not to cry, dreaming of the perfect Melody-made computer. First of all, it would talk! Oh, yes. People would have to tell me to shut up! And it would have room to store *all* my words, not just the most common ones that have gotten pasted on my dumb plastic board.

It would have big keys, so my thumbs could push the right buttons, and it would connect to my wheelchair. It would not have to be lime green.

I open my eyes with a start. Such a thing *has* to exist, right? Or something like it? Maybe?

I grab Catherine's arm and point to Rose's computer. **Me too,** I punch on my board. I do it several times.

"You want a computer like Rose's?" Catherine glances over at Rose's laptop. "It really is nice. Even I don't have one as cool as hers."

No, I point.

"Wait, you don't want a computer?" Catherine sounds confused.

I have learned to be patient with people. Once again I point to Rose's computer and then to the words **me too.** I search all over my communication board, and the words *better, nicer,* and *cooler* just aren't there. So I point to **good,** then go to the alphabet strip and then jab at the letters **E** and **R**. **Good-er.** I sound like a doofus.

"Oh!" Catherine says finally. "You want a better computer than Rose's?"

Yes! I pound on the board. Then I point to **for** and **me**.

"I get it!" Catherine cried. "You want something specially designed for you! That's just plain brilliant, Melody!"

I spell out **D-U-H**, and we laugh.

Miss Gordon starts class then, reminding everyone about due dates for the biography project.

"Tomorrow," she announces, "class will meet in the media center so that you can make final choices about the person you will write about. And next week we will begin making outlines of your life stories. Any questions?"

Connor, always the class clown, raises his hand. "I found out the guy who invented the flush toilet was named Thomas Crapper. Can I do my report on him?"

Kids crack up. Rodney laughs so hard, his whole face turned red.

Miss Gordon shushes Rodney and the others. "Sorry, Connor. I get this request every year. The flush toilet was invented in 1596 by John Harrington. No funny name. Do you still want to research him?"

Connor looks deflated. "Nah, I guess I'll stay with the folks who started McDonald's. If I've got to spend a lot of time looking up stuff, burgers are better than toilets."

Rodney tries to bust out laughing again, but Miss Gordon silences him with a look.

"Who will you choose to write about?" Catherine asks me as Miss Gordon walks around the class talking to students about their projects.

I think for only a minute. **S-T-E-P-H-E-N H-A-W-K-I-N-G**, I spell out.

I want to know how he does ordinary stuff, like eating and drinking. After all, he's a grown man. Does his wife put him on the toilet? He has kids. How does he manage to be a dad?

And I want to know about his talking devices, the supercool computers that help him talk and do really hard math problems, like finding black holes in space.

I tap out the question for Catherine: **Computer for me?**

"I have no idea!" she replies. "Let's check it out."

CHAPTER 15

The next morning we get the first snowfall of the season. Big, fat flakes fall outside the windows of room H-5.

Freddy zooms over and touches the window. "Nice," he says.

Mrs. Shannon rolls all of us closer so we can watch the snow accumulate on the grass and trees. It's really pretty. Even Jill seems to relax.

"We gonna play in the snow?" asks Maria.

"No, Maria. It's too cold to play outside, but guess what? It's gettin' close to Christmas!"

Maria cheers.

"I've heard it's some sort of a tradition round here to decorate this old Styrofoam snowman," Mrs. Shannon continues. She makes a face as she pulls Sydney's head out of his box.

Maria starts to hug it, but Mrs. Shannon stops her and says, "I believe in the smell of fresh pine trees at holiday time, and real candy canes, and popcorn garland. Tomorrow I'm bringing in a real tree and we're going to make it beautiful!"

Freddy and Carl slap palms. Maria looks disappointed for a moment, but she seems to forget about the snowman as Mrs. Shannon gives everyone a soft piece of chocolate candy. She wisely stuffs Sydney back into his box.

While Mrs. Shannon shows the rest of the class how to make paper snowflakes, Catherine and I sit together in front of the one clunky classroom computer and do Web searches on communication devices. It's soooo slow. Sometimes it gets jammed up and stalls, and we have to reboot it and start all over. Room H-5 always gets the big old leftover computers that the other classrooms no longer want.

Catherine and I research all kinds of electronic talking and communication devices that have been designed for people like me. Lots of them seem as clunky and awkward as our room computer. Some look really complicated. All of them are expensive. Crazy expensive. Some of the websites don't even list the prices — like they're afraid to specify how much the things cost.

The devices that use standard computer

keyboards wouldn't work. I'd have no way to hit the individual keys. I need something that would work with just my thumbs.

We find adapted computers, talking boards that speak the words, push-button systems, and even devices that work with blinks or head nods. Finally, we find something called a Medi-Talker that looks like a possibility. It has spaces big enough for my thumbs to get into and millions of words and phrases built into it!

I watch an online video of a boy about my age using one, and even though he clearly has no voice of his own, this little box lets him tell all the details of his recent birthday party! I get so excited that my legs start kicking and my arms start flailing and I look like some kind of crazy human helicopter.

Catherine prints out the information and tucks it into the book bag that is attached to the back of my chair. "Good luck, Melody!" she whispers as she leaves for the day.

When I get off the bus after school, Mrs. V is waiting for me as usual. I almost twist out of my seat trying to point to my bag to let her know I have something important in it.

"Hold your horses!" Mrs. V says. "Since when are you excited to do homework? What's got you all in a tizzy today?"

I just grin and kick. After my snack of caramel candy (first) and tuna melt (last), and after Penny, who has just gotten up from her nap, eats her applesauce, Mrs. V *finally* pulls the papers out of my bag.

"Well, this is *exactly* what you need," Mrs. V says, slapping the printouts onto the table after reading them. "No wonder you're all fired up."

Yes! Yes! Yes! I point. Then I point to the individual words: **Talk. To. Mom. And. Dad. Talk. Talk. Talk.**

"I'll do just that, just as soon as they get home from work, Melody," Mrs. V promises.

I can hardly wait. While Penny watches Cookie Monster gobble carrots instead of cookies on *Sesame Street,* I dream of talking, talking, talking.

When Mom picks us up, Mrs. V, true to her word, not only shows Mom the printouts, but even has her computer already set to the Web page where the Medi-Talker is advertised and sold. Penny sits on Mom's lap and keeps pushing computer keys, messing up the display, which is getting on my nerves. But Mom watches the video that shows people actually talking and cracking jokes and even going to college by using that machine.

Mrs. V explains to Mom how this is

exactly right for me, and Mom, instead of being practical and sensible and thrifty like she usually is, seems to agree.

"Looks like insurance will cover about half the cost," she muses as she navigates the website. "Let me talk to Chuck. This is long overdue."

Tonight? I ask from my board.

"Yep! Tonight!" Mom says, giving me a squeeze.

But nothing happens right away in my world. Mom fills out the online application for the machine the next day and sends it in. I wait.

Then we have to ask my doctor to fax in a prescription. I've heard of prescriptions for antibiotics, but for machines? That seems crazy. Who'd ever want this machine unless they needed it? I wait.

Next, we have to get approval from our insurance company. More paperwork and phone calls, more questions and answers. I wait.

A parental financial statement has to be turned in. You gotta be kidding! Why do they make it so complicated? I wait.

The medical form was missing one signature and has to be resubmitted. I wait.

One last approval form from a school official has to be turned in. I wait.

144

I realize I've been waiting for this thing all my life.

Finally, finally, finally, on the Wednesday before Christmas, the Medi-Talker arrives. I need no other gift.

When I get home from school, Mrs. V tells me that she hurried to my house when she saw the UPS truck pulling up in our driveway. She signed for the package and brought it to her house for safekeeping. The huge brown box sits there taped and secure. And it is addressed to *me*!

I wiggle and squeal and insist we open it right away. I can feel one of my tornadoes coming on. *Spastic City, here I come!*

"Calm down, Mello Yello," Mrs. V says, placing a hand on my shoulder, but I can't relax.

Open! Open! Open! I tap.

"Well, your mom knew you'd be impatient," Mrs. V says, "so when I called her to say it arrived, she told me it was okay for us to open it."

I feel like I'm going to have a heart attack watching Mrs. V carefully open the edges of the box. She lets me pull at the brown paper inside. Then, under about a mile of bubble wrap, there it is. The Medi-Talker. Smaller than I expected, it's only the size of my wheelchair tray, but it's sleek and shiny and

145

cool to the touch. It is like a butterfly ready to unfold its wings.

Boy, oh, boy. I can't wait to try it.

Mrs. V plugs it into a wall outlet to charge the battery, then pulls out the *huge* booklet of directions. "Whew!" she says. "This will take a year to read and understand." She flops down in a soft easy chair with Penny on her lap and begins to read.

And I begin to wait. And wait. And wait. Finally, when I just know I'm going to explode, I wheel over to the table where the Medi-Talker sits.

I've seen the kids at school play video games they've never seen before, and I've seen them program their phones and computers without touching a book of instructions. So I take my right thumb and push the on button. The board whirs and glows, and then a welcome message appears on the screen.

I push another button, and a voice that sounds like an Englishman with a really bad head cold blurts out, **"Welcome to Medi-Talker!"**

Mrs. V jumps up from the couch. I shriek with joy. "It looks like you're way ahead of me, Melody. Not that I'm surprised." She sets Penny down. "Now let's see what this machine can do!"

146

I feel like Christopher Columbus bumping into America. It had been there all the time, but he was the first one from his world to find it. I wonder if his heart had beat as fast as mine is.

We quickly discover that the Medi-Talker has more than a dozen levels, all easily reached with just one button. So on level one we program in the names of everyone I know — my name, all the members of my family, kids and teachers at school, my doctors, the neighbors, my parents' friends, and, of course, Mrs. V. On the second level she insists we add all the vocabulary words we've been collecting on our multicolored three-by-five-inch flash cards.

Type, save. Type, save. Mrs. V's fingers fly as she keeps adding words for me. Lots of our vocabulary words are already in the machine's memory, but she gives me more. More. More.

Nouns, verbs, adverbs, and adjectives — thousands of them — as well as a cool sentence-maker that is located on another level. We can prepare hundreds of phrases and sentences and get to them with just a touch.

Have you heard their latest song?
That's what's up!
How did you do on the spelling test?

Ordinary words. Normal conversation. I've never had that. Awesome.

Another level is for numbers and even computation — I'll be able to do math now. Maybe I won't tell the teachers about that one.

And there's a level full of corny jokes and silly sayings, with room left for us to add more. Another level plays music! I can connect the device to a computer and download any song I want. I can't wait to search iTunes. Maybe I can ask Rose which songs are hot.

Rose! I can actually talk to Rose now!

We stop programming after a while. Penny needs to be changed and kept occupied. But I'm much too excited to rest.

So after Mrs. V gets Penny set up with her dollhouse at the foot of the couch, we add even more words and phrases. Finally, she stops typing and says, "Would you like to try it out?"

The room is absolutely quiet. I stroke the edge of the machine softly, then push two buttons.

"Thanks, Mrs. V," the computer's voice says.

She blinks real fast. I do too. She reaches for a tissue. We both need it.

Mrs. V tucks the tissue into her pocket,

then begins reading again from the instruction manual. "Hey, listen to this!" she says. "With that connector cord, you can also save longer things you want to write — like stories or poems — on the computer!"

"**Wow**," the machine says.

Mrs. V nods in agreement. "This is going to be fun. But you're gonna need lots of practice to make it say what you want, kid."

She's right.

Many levels have been left blank for users to input their own information — words, sentences, phone numbers, even pictures. Information can be typed directly into the machine, or it can be downloaded from a computer. It's a little overwhelming.

"We can design this to fit *you,* Melody," Mrs. V tells me. "This will be *your* world, so let's take our time and make it exactly what you need."

I am so happy — I almost feel like hugging the machine, but that would look silly. Instead, I name it. That's probably pretty dumb, but sometimes it's good to have something that nobody else knows but you. I'm not going to type the name into the machine, because it's personal, but in my mind I'm going to call the Medi-Talker "Elvira," after that song I like. Yep, my heart's on fire for Elvira!

While Mrs. V plays with Penny for a while, I continue to explore what Elvira can do. One of the first changes I want to make is the hello message and the voice that speaks it. The computer-produced greeting sounds really fake. But the machine offers several female voices to choose from, as well as a bunch of different languages.

I pick the voice called "Trish." She actually sounds like a girl, not a grown-up. I wouldn't mind sounding like her if I could talk.

"Bienvenue," Trish says in French. I know that means "welcome." I push the button for German and she says, *"Willkommen."* I even find something that sounds like *"Foon ying"* when I touch the button for Chinese.

I stop for a minute and stare at the board. It has never occurred to me that there are kids like me in Germany and China and France who need a machine to help them talk.

Mrs. V returns to me and helps me change the original welcome message from the very mechanical-sounding **"Welcome to Medi-Talker"** to Trish's voice saying, **"Hi! I'm Melody. Talk to me!"** I can't wait to take it to school and introduce *my* new computer to everybody there. I wonder what Rose will say.

By now both Mom and Dad have called to check on how we're doing, how much progress we've made. They're both anxious to get here and see the device for themselves, so while we wait, Mrs. V suggests that we just keep programming it, adding more and more. She thinks I should practice using it for a couple of weeks before taking it to school. I don't really want to wait, but I have to agree with her that this is going to take some time. I want to be able to use the system to talk like ordinary kids. Sort of.

So we return to words — I want to input thousands of them: *Notebook. Marker. Homework. Assignment. Test. Positive. Negative. Fingernail. Nail polish. Outfit. Backpack. Purse. Scared. Excited. Purple.*

Then we type in more phrases — hundreds of them: *to the mall, from a distance, in the middle of, as a result, the reason why.*

Lastly, we get to some sentences — dozens of them: *What time is it? What's up with that? You crack me up. I'm so excited.* — before the doorbell rings.

When Dad and Mom come in to pick us up, Dad is ready with his camcorder. His hands are shaking a little. "Show us how it works, honey," he says.

I can't believe Dad is making a video of me saying my first words. It's almost like when he filmed Penny's first words — well, not really.

I type very carefully and push the button to make the machine speak.

"Hi, Dad. Hi, Mom. I am so happy."

Mom gets all teary-eyed, and her nose gets red. She is looking at me all soft and gooey.

When I think about it, I realize I have never, ever said any words directly to my parents. So I push a couple of buttons, and the machine speaks the words I've never been able to say.

"I love you."

Mom completely loses it. She bubbles up with tears and grabs Dad. I think he might be sniffing back a couple of tears himself.

But he has recorded it all.

CHAPTER 16

I wait until after the holiday break to take the machine into school. I have practiced with Mrs. V every single day of Christmas vacation. Learning how to push the right buttons, how to switch smoothly from one level to another, how to make contractions. I had to figure out how to say *isn't* instead of *is not,* or *there's* instead of *there is.* It was hard. I kept messing up, but Mrs. V wouldn't let me quit. I didn't want to.

So on that first Monday back, Elvira is the star of the day, making me the center of attention. And not because of something embarrassing I did, like throwing up or spilling my food, but for something really cool instead. Unbelievable!

Even the teachers seem impressed. "Watch out, world!" Mrs. Shannon announces when she sees me in the hallway. "Melody is ready to rock, y'all!"

I grin, push a button, and a song from the

latest teen musical begins to play.

"Girl, you really got it goin' on! Music and everything!" Mrs. Shannon starts sashaying down the hall in rhythm to my music. I crack up.

In room H-5, Maria is glued to me all morning. "Cool beans, Melly-Belly," she keeps repeating. "Cool beans. Can I play?" She wants to touch the glowing lights and shiny buttons, but Mrs. Shannon steps in and distracts her with a new computer game she's loaded on the classroom machine.

When Catherine comes in, just before the bell for language arts class, I'm ready for her. She's wearing a green plaid shirt, a blue skirt, and orange knee socks. I planned the first thing I wanted to say to her, so Mrs. V and I had programmed it in ahead of time. I push a button and smile. **"Let's go shopping."**

Catherine gasps, then laughs so hard, she almost can't catch her breath. Then she runs over to me and hugs me. "I'm so happy for you, Melody! You really needed this! And, yes, we're gonna have to find a day so you can teach me some fashion sense!"

"We need hurry," I type in. I am in a great mood.

"You're a coldhearted woman!" Catherine declares, still laughing. "But for now, let's

154

get you to your inclusion classes and show off this cool new machine!"

I shiver with excitement. When I roll into Miss Gordon's room, as usual, nobody looks up, except for Rose, who flashes me a smile.

But then I turn the volume up real loud and I push a button: **"Hi, everybody. I have a new computer."**

Heads turn and voices whisper.

"They make computers for the special eddies?"

"It talks? Mine doesn't do that."

"You don't *need* yours to talk!"

"It sounds weird."

"So do you."

"What could she possibly have to say, anyway?"

But Connor jumps up, his shaggy blond hair flopping into his eyes, and says loudly, "That's awesome, Melody!"

And because he's one of the popular kids, and probably the biggest and tallest kid in the fifth grade, I think because he gives his okay, the rest of the students decide to leave it alone.

Well, most of them. Claire, who was the first in the class to get her own laptop and who makes sure everybody knows it when she gets a new iPhone or a Wii game, sniffs and says, "That sure is a funny-looking computer! But I guess it's perfect for a kid like you." She and Molly exchange looks. I swear they think I am blind.

Miss Gordon, who looks like she wants to squeeze Claire like an empty toothpaste tube, tells her, "Claire, I don't allow rudeness in my classroom. Now sit down and hush!"

But even Claire can't dim my good mood. I push another button for a sentence Mrs. V and I prepared ahead of time. Somehow I knew I would need it! The machine says, **"I talk to everybody now — Claire, too!"**

I see her scowl, but everyone else laughs. They all want to touch the machine or push a button or try to operate it, but Catherine keeps them away and lets me do all the demonstrating.

I go to the green level — the jokes. **"Knock, knock!"**

"Who's there?" several people reply together.

"Isabel," the Medi-Talker says.

"Isabel who?" the kids surrounding me reply.

"Isabel out of order? I had to knock!"

Everybody laughs at the silly joke with me. Even though my arms and legs flail out and I drool a little as I laugh, it is the first time

156

in my entire life that I feel like I'm part of the group.

I wish I could click a save button so I could play this moment over and over and over again.

I type in, **"Today is Monday. It is cold,"** then push a blue button on the machine. It whirs a little, then, like a tongue sticking out, a thin sheet of paper erupts from the side of it. Printed on it are the words I just typed.

"Whoa!" says Rodney, the champion video game player in the class. "It's got a printer! That's too slick!"

Miss Gordon nods with encouragement as Catherine passes the printout around so everyone can read my words. Then Catherine tells the class, "Melody's Medi-Talker is a combination computer, music player, and speech device. It's got HD, high-tech guts, and it's designed to rock her world and connect you to it. Take the time to listen to what she has to say."

Claire raises her hand.

"Yes, Claire," Miss Gordon says, a look of warning in her eyes.

"I'm not trying to be mean — honest — but it just never occurred to me that Melody had thoughts in her head."

A couple of other kids nod slightly.

Miss Gordon doesn't raise her voice. Instead, she responds thoughtfully: "You've always been able to say whatever came to your mind, Claire. All of you. But Melody has been forced to be silent. She probably has mountains of stuff to say."

"Yes. Yes. Yes," I make the machine say.

I give Miss Gordon a smile of thanks, then I show Rodney and Connor a video game that came with my Medi-Talker. I doubt if I'll ever be fast enough to play Space Soldiers, but it's nice to know it's there. Rodney could probably master it in a hot minute.

Miss Gordon checks out the various levels and looks impressed. "What a huge vocabulary you have now, Melody!" she says to me. "I know you feel like a ton of bricks have been lifted from you."

I nod. **"Way cold,"** the machine says loudly. Oops! I meant to say *Way cool.* I feel my face getting warm as I hear Claire and Molly snicker.

But Rose pulls her desk close to my chair. "This is so awesome, Melody," she says softly, and I let her touch the shimmery keys.

"Oh, yes," I reply. Then I look at her. **"Friends?"** I type.

"Friends!" she answers without hesitation.

158

"Happy," I type, then I tense. I hope I won't do anything stupid like knock something over with excitement.

Rose is looking intently at me. "I can't imagine what it must be like to have all my words stuck inside," she finally says.

"It sucks!" I type in.

Rose chuckles. "I feel you!"

CHAPTER 17

As I've been getting used to using Elvira over the last month, life at school has been almost pleasant. Almost. I can ask Connor about a TV show that came on the night before or tell Jessica that I like her new shoes.

It's been snowing — just flurries — almost every day. Late one January afternoon I typed, **"I hope we have a snow day — no school."** Everybody agreed. For once, I got to speak for the class.

I can answer questions in class lots better with Elvira to help me. For the first time, instead of "pretend" grades that teachers would give me because they weren't quite sure if I knew the answer or not, I get real grades recorded in the teachers' grade books that are based on actual answers I've given. Printed out and everything!

But at recess I still sit alone. It's been too cold to go outside, so we sit in the far corner of the overheated cafeteria until it's time to go back to class. None of the girls gossip with me about some silly thing a boy has said. Nobody promises to call me after school. Nobody asks me to come to a birthday party or a sleepover. Not even Rose.

Sure, she'll stop and chat for a minute or two, but as soon as Janice or Paula calls her to come and look at a picture on a cell phone, Rose will say, "I'll be right back!" then skip away as if she's glad she has a reason to cut out on me.

I just smile, hope I wasn't drooling, and pretend I didn't notice. After a few minutes of faking it, I push the button for the sentence **"Go back to H-5,"** and Catherine and I roll back down the hall.

One afternoon near the end of January, Mr. Dimming announced, in a voice that sounded like he'd been chewing on dry toast, "Instead of regular class today, I think we'll have a practice round for the Whiz Kids quiz team."

Everybody cheered because, otherwise, we would have had a lesson on the Sahara Desert. Talk about toasty and dry!

Every year our school sends a team to the Whiz Kids competition. The local rounds, with teams from elementary schools all around the city and county, are held downtown at a hotel. Last year our school got to second place in the whole district. The principal was so proud, she bought pizza for the entire school, even though the team was only for grades four, and five and six.

The first-place teams from across the state go to Washington, D.C., for the nationals. It's televised and is a really big deal.

Rose scooted her desk closer to mine. "I was on the Whiz Kids team last year," she told me.

"I know," I typed. **"You're smart."**

She beamed, then leaned closer. "Connor will probably get picked again too. He's a little hard to handle, but he's great with trivia."

I glanced over — Connor was boasting to his friends about last year's competition. "You ought to *see* the room in the hotel where they hold the contest. Gold chandeliers! Rich-looking stuff everywhere! And kids from all over looking smart. But we smoked them all!"

"All but one team, dude," Rodney shouted out good-naturedly. "They tore you up!" The class hooted.

"Yeah, but this year we're gonna win! Right, Mr. D?"

"We're certainly going to try, Connor,"

162

Mr. Dimming replied. "The rules have changed slightly, so our team this year will be made up of just grades five and six. That gives us strength because some of you competed last year. Now let's just see how good we are. Let's do a set of sample questions just for fun, shall we?"

"You got prizes?" Rodney asked.

"Not every competition results in a prize, Rodney," Mr. D replied.

"Yeah, but it's more fun with good stuff at the end," Connor added. "Please?"

"Okay, okay! One slightly squished Butterfinger candy bar from my lunch bag," the teacher said, holding it up. Everyone laughed once more.

"Chocolate gives you zits," Rose teased Connor. "I don't want candy — I want to win!" She moved her desk back to her own row.

Catherine sat on the other side of me. "Do you want to play the practice round with them?" she asked.

"Yes! Yes! Yes!" I typed. **"Answers — A, B, C, D. Easy."**

She grinned. "Okay, easy! Let's see what happens!"

Mr. Dimming cleared his throat and smiled. "Whiz Kids time is my favorite event of the year," he admitted. "Let's see if we can go all the way this year!"

The class cheered.

"I will read the questions first, then the choices for the answers. You will write down the correct letter. Does everyone understand?"

Connor raised his hand, then called out even before Mr. Dimming noticed him. "Don't give us easy ones, Mr. D. I've got brains of steel!"

"And a mouth to match," I heard Rose whisper.

"Number one," the teacher began. "Which planet is closest to the sun?
A. Venus
B. Earth
C. Mercury
D. Mars
E. Jupiter."

"Baby questions!" Connor protested.

"Please, Connor. Silence," Mr. D said sternly. Connor finally shut up.

I pushed the letter *C* on my machine and waited for the next question.

"Number two," Mr. Dimming continued. "How many sides are on a heptagon?
A. Four
B. Six
C. Seven
D. Eight

164

E. Nine."

I typed in the letter *C* again. Would the same letter come up twice in a row? Why not? I knew I was right.

"Question number three," Mr. D. said. "How long is one regular term for a U.S. representative?

A. One year

B. Two years

C. Three years

D. Four years

E. Six years."

Hmmm. That one could be tricky. It seems like the same politicians are on the news all the time. But I typed in *B* as my answer.

Mr. D gave us fifty questions in all. Several were math problems. Others had to do with science and grammar. The last question was about geography.

"In what state would you find the Grand Canyon?" he asked.

A. California

B. Arizona

C. South Dakota

D. New Mexico

E. Utah."

I've never been there, but I've seen specials on the Travel Channel, and I'm almost positive it's in Arizona. I typed in the letter *B*, pushed the print button, and Catherine took my paper to the teacher's desk.

"Melody participated?" Mr. Dimming asked as he took the printout. He glanced from me to the paper in his hand. "How nice."

I didn't like the sound of his voice.

He scored the papers while we watched a movie about the pyramids in Egypt. I couldn't help stealing glances at him.

Finally, Mr. Dimming looked over his wire-rimmed glasses. "I've tallied the results. These are not official tryouts, but the students with very high scores today are Paula, Claire, Rose, and Connor."

Connor jumped from his desk and cheered. "I knew it! I'm the man! I'm hot! Lemme hold that piece of candy!" He started up the aisle toward the desk where the Butterfinger lay.

"Sit down, Connor!" the teacher said with exasperation. "You did well, but you don't get the candy."

"Who beat me?" Connor seemed amazed. "Rose? That's okay. I'll triumph in the real tryouts."

I looked over at Rose. She smiled at me — a look of anticipation on her face.

Mr. Dimming was silent for a moment. He scratched his head. Finally, he cleared

166

his throat and said, "The winner of today's competition, and the winner of the Butterfinger candy bar, with a *perfect* score, is . . ." He paused again, gave his head a shake, and started again. "The only person in the class who got every single question correct is . . . Melody Brooks."

Dead silence. No cheers. Just looks of disbelief.

"No fair!" Molly blurted out angrily. "Melody's got a helper who whispers the answers to her!"

"She musta cheated!" Claire added loudly.

Catherine jumped out of her chair and stormed over to where Claire and Molly were sitting, her new black leather boots clicking sharply on the tiled classroom floor. "I did *not* help her! Did it ever occur to you that she might have some smarts of her own?"

"She can't even sit up by herself!" Claire replied, her voice petulant.

"What your body looks like has nothing to do with how well your brain works! You ought to know that by looking in the mirror!"

"Ooh! She got you!" Connor said. That got a couple of laughs. But most of the kids were looking around uneasily. No one looked at me.

Claire said nothing in reply, and I guess Molly decided to shut up as well.

Catherine returned to where I sat, but the whole thing made me want to crawl under a table and disappear.

Mr. Dimming raised his hand for the class to be silent. "Melody, please come up and get your candy bar," he said. "I am very proud of you and your efforts today. And your classmates are as well. Let's all give Melody a round of applause!"

Everybody, except maybe Molly and Claire, clapped as I rolled slowly to the front of the room. The sound of my chair's motor whirred softly. They couldn't hear the sound of my thumping heart.

I figured the teacher offered me the candy to shut up Claire and Molly and to make me feel good that I accidentally got all the questions right. But it was no accident. I knew them all. Every single one.

Mr. Dimming placed the candy bar on my tray. Good. At least I wouldn't have to worry about dropping it in front of everybody. I rolled back to my place with my head down.

"I'm so proud of you! And you should be too!" Catherine whispered, holding her hand up for me to slap. But I didn't move.

"Not," I typed.

"Why not? You beat them all."

It took me a very long time, but I typed, **"They think my brain is messed up like the rest of me."** I felt like crying.

"Then we'll just have to study and show them they're wrong!" Catherine said, a hint of defiance edging her voice.

"Why?" I asked.

"So you can be on the quiz team," she told me.

"Never happen," I tapped.

Just as Catherine was about to reply, Mr. Dimming announced that the official try-outs for the quiz team would be held in one week. "Many of you scored quite well on this practice round," he said, "but remember you will have to compete against the sixth-grade students as well for the real competition. Go home and study. Only the best will be chosen."

"Like me?" Connor yelled.

"If you qualify," Mr. Dimming told him. "I'm taking a winning team to Washington, D.C., this year, class. Are you with me?"

"Yeah!" they all yelled.

I was amazed they'd get excited about studying for anything. But he rallied them like a football coach.

"Are you willing to study so we can be on television?"

"Oh, yeah!"

"You gonna buy a new suit if we win?" Connor blurted out.

Mr. Dimming actually laughed. "That's a promise. A new suit — maybe blue — with a red satin vest."

The whole class broke out in laughter and applause.

"Then, let's do our very best," Mr. D said. "I'm going to create extra-challenging questions so that we will be stupendously prepared this year."

"Well, he's already starting with the big vocabulary words," I heard Molly whisper to Claire.

"Hard questions?" Connor whined.

"Look at it this way," Mr. Dimming told Connor. "If Melody Brooks can win the first round, then my questions must not be difficult enough! We're all going to rally to win the competition!"

Everybody cheered.

Except me.

CHAPTER 18

After school that day I was grumpy and mean. Mrs. V had prepared a new stack of word cards for me. Penny was wearing one of Mrs. V's turbans, and she looked ridiculous. Plus, she kept singing some stupid baby song at the top of her lungs. I took my arm and swept the whole pile of cards to the floor.

"Who put salt in your Kool-Aid, Miss Thing?" Mrs. V asked. She did not pick up the cards.

Penny stopped singing and stood there blinking at me.

I switched the Medi-Talker to off and looked away.

"Fine. Be like that. But you're going to pick up every single one of those cards!"

I stuck out my lip and stared at the wall.

Penny reached out and shook my arm. I tugged it loose. She didn't seem to care and started singing again:

171

"Happy, happy, happy, clap your feet,
Happy, sappy, pappy, blow your nose,
Biddy-boddy-bowdee, jump and jump."

She jumped. She stomped her feet. Then she sang the song again. And again.

She was really getting on my nerves. I wished she would just shut up! Talking all the time. Walking all the time. Jumping and bouncing and singing. *Just quit it! For just one moment, please STOP!*

But she wouldn't. "Hi, Dee-Dee," she said. She put Doodle on my tray.

I pushed the toy to the floor.

"Doodle, Dee-Dee." She picked up the stupid raggedy thing and placed it on my tray once more.

I knocked it off again. *Leave me alone!* I wanted to scream.

Penny was used to things falling off my chair, so she couldn't know I was being just plain horrible. The third time she put Doodle on my tray, I swept it off with such force that my arm brushed Penny's head. She toppled over and fell to the floor.

She looked at me, surprise on her face, grabbed Doodle, and ran to Mrs. V in tears.

"What's gotten into you, Melody?" Mrs. V asked as she rocked Penny on her lap.

How could I explain?

I didn't want to cry, but I did. I turned

my wheel-chair so it faced the wall just as the phone rang. Mrs. V looked from me to the phone, sighed, and got up to answer it.

"Oh, hello, Catherine."

Catherine? I turned my chair slightly to listen better.

"Out of sorts?" Mrs. V asked. "Well, as a matter of fact, she does seem a little mopey this afternoon. No, I take that back. She's downright monstrous." Mrs. V caught my eye and made a funny face at me.

I just glared at her.

"I'm not surprised she got all the questions right — the child is brilliant!"

Lotta good it does me.

"The teacher said *what?*"

Great, now *everybody* would know. Just thinking about it made me feel like pond scum again.

"In front of her classmates? What kind of professional is he supposed to be?" Mrs. V looked furious.

"How did she react? Never mind. I already know. She's sitting here looking like one of those blowfish we saw at the aquarium — all puffed up and spiny."

That's actually kinda close to how I felt.

"Thanks so much for calling, Catherine," Mrs. V said. "Yes, please call her parents this evening, and I'll be sure to talk to them as well. I am going to work on this problem right now."

With that, she hung up the phone, set Penny down on the floor, put her hands on her hips, and turned to look at me.

I figured here's where she hugs me and makes me feel better.

"So, you aced the quiz and then bombed the follow-up?" she said to me, indignation decorating her words. She flipped my talker back on.

Why did she sound mad at *me*? I looked up in surprise.

"He hurt my feelings," I answered.

"So what?" Mrs. V spat back.

"Kids laughed. Even Rose." It was true, though I could hardly admit it. Even Rose had covered her mouth to stifle a laugh.

"Did you get the highest score in the class?" Mrs. V asked, completely ignoring my attempt to make her feel sorry for me. I should have known better.

"Yes."

"Did Catherine help you in any way — even a little bit?"

"No."

"Then let's get started."

I looked at her, a little confused. **"Started on what?"** I asked.

"On your study plan. You and I are going

174

to practice, prepare, and push. I am going to quiz you, and you are going to answer. We're going to learn geography, science, math — thousands of glorious tidbits of information!"

She sounded excited.

"Why?" I asked carefully.

"You know how athletes get ready for the Olympics? They swim early in the morning and late at night. They run around the track for hours and hours without a crowd to cheer them on."

"I can't run very fast," I typed, then I grinned at her.

"Maybe not, but you've got the fastest, strongest brain in that school, and you are going to try out for the quiz team next week."

"They won't let me be on the team," I typed slowly.

"Oh, yes they will! They'll want you, all right. They'll *need* you, Melody. You are going to be their secret weapon."

"You think?"

"I know. Now let's cut out all this fake feeling sorry for yourself and get started on studying. We have one week. I'm the coach, and you're my athlete. Get ready to sweat!"

"Sweat stinks!" I told her with a laugh.

"So let's get stinky! But first you are going to pick up every single one of those cards."

I knew not to argue. She took me out of my chair, set me on the floor, and left the room while I pulled the cards that I'd knocked down into a messy pile on the floor. Penny helped.

Then Mrs. V put me back in my chair, and we got to work. She was gonna be a tough coach. "How is the test set up?" she asked me.

"A, B, C, D," I tapped.

"Multiple choice! Wonderful! Piece of cake for you."

I wasn't sure about that, but I didn't disagree with her.

She went to her computer and found a Web page that listed every U.S. state and capital.

"Did those in school," I told her.

"Great! So we'll do them again!"

I fake groaned.

Mrs. V then looked up the capitals of all the major countries in the world. Gee, there sure are a *lot* of countries! But once she read them out loud to me, I had the info stuck in my head.

"What's the capital of Hungary?" she demanded.

I knew the answer was Budapest before

176

she even gave me the four choices.

"A. Accra

B. Berlin

C. New Delhi

D. Budapest."

I pushed *D,* of course. Mrs. V didn't stop to cheer. She kept going.

I correctly answered that Tokyo was the capital of Japan, Addis Ababa the capital of Ethiopia, Ottawa the capital of Canada, and Bogotá the capital of Colombia. She quizzed me until Dad came to pick us up.

As Mrs. V stuffed Doodle and some unused diapers back into Penny's bag, she explained briefly what had happened at school and what she planned to do about it, what we were already doing.

"Are you sure?" Dad asked, glancing at me. "Maybe we're setting her up for failure, and she'll be hurt even worse."

"I am absolutely positive!" Mrs. V insisted. "Can Melody stay a little longer to study? I'll give her dinner and bring her home in a couple of hours. That will give you some one-on-one time with Penny."

"You cool with that?" Dad asked me.

"Yes! Yes! Yes!" I typed. **"I want to do this."**

"Go for it, my Melody," Dad said. He gave

Mrs. V a thumbs-up sign and left with Penny.

After dinner we moved on to science. I learned that the bones in the leg are the femur, the tibia, the patella, and the fibula. Why can't they just call them something easy, like "knee bone" and "skinny leg bone"? But I memorized them.

I learned that insects are arthropods and that they have tibias too!

"The study of insects is called 'entomology,' " Mrs. V said. "That gives me an idea — let's learn all the words that end in 'ology'!"

I put my hand over my head and pretended to groan, but deep inside I was really jazzed.

"Which word means the study of words and their meanings?" she asked me after we had reviewed a very long list of "ology" words.

"A. Bibliography
B. Archeology
C. Histology
D. Lexicology."

I thought for a minute. I knew she was trying to trick me. *Histology* sounds like *history,* but for some reason, I think it has to do with skin. And *bibliography* has to do with books, not words. I typed in the letter

D.

This time she did cheer. "Let me get you home, Melody. Top athletes need their sleep. We'll do some more tomorrow."

I grinned at her, tired and energized at the same time.

Mrs. V had called Catherine and explained the situation, told her to stuff information into my head along with the macaroni at lunch. So the next morning Catherine, of course, jumped right in.

While we were in room H-5, Catherine hooked me up on the earphones. I listened to an old audio cassette on volcanoes. It was scratchy and skipped a little, but it gave me information. Volcanoes were named for the Roman god Vulcan. I could've figured that one out myself. I found out about lava and ash. I learned about how the whole city of Pompeii got covered up when Vesuvius erupted. Surprisingly interesting stuff.

I listened to tapes on Australia and Russia, on constellations and on the planets.

"You learning anything from these oldies but goodies?" Catherine asked as she slipped in another tape for me. It was on diseases.

"Info always good," I typed.

"I feel you," she replied. "Are you still upset about what happened in Mr. Dim-

179

ming's class?"

"Deleted the memory — need room for facts," I took the time to type.

She gave me a thumbs-up.

"I'm a little scared," I admitted. **"Suppose I mess up?"**

"You can do this, Melody," she said sternly as she adjusted the earphones. "You certainly have enough smarts to be on the team."

"Go away while I take the test," I typed. **"Keeps Claire quiet."**

"Gotcha!" Catherine said. She held her hand up to slap my palm. It wasn't much of a slap — more like a mushy grab — but we were on the same page.

Except for lunch and recess, I listened to tapes and worked with Catherine the rest of the day. She quizzed me on facts and dates and kings. And math. That might be hard for me. Words float easily into my head. But numbers seem to sink to the bottom like rocks. I don't know why.

"Let's do it again," Catherine said gently as I got mixed up on a math problem about trains and their speed.

Nobody rides trains anymore! Who cares?

But she kept at it until it made sense to me. I discovered that if I make numbers into a picture story in my mind, the answers

180

come easier. I changed the figures to words. Magic!

Instead of going out for inclusion classes, I shook my head and told Catherine I didn't want to go. I wanted to stay and study instead.

Evidently, I wasn't missed. Nobody sent a frantic message to room H-5, wondering why Melody wasn't in class today. Nobody peeked their head in the door to see if I was absent or sick or maybe having a convulsion in the middle of the floor.

Nobody seemed to notice at all.

CHAPTER 19

The week zipped by. I studied at school every day with Catherine, after school every day with Mrs. V, and every evening at home as well. I reviewed words from all the levels of my board. I practiced spelling long words and matching facts and dates. I made up my own games. Mom quizzed me about flowers and medical terms. Dad asked me questions about economics and retail management and sports. I swallowed it all.

Sometimes I sit in my room and just type in new sentences for Elvira to say. One letter at a time. It takes hours. But once an entry is in, all I have to do is push one button and the whole sentence will be spoken for me.

I guess the question I get asked the most, in a lot of strange variations, is: "What's wrong with you?" People often want to know if I'm sick or if I'm in pain or if my condition can be fixed. So I prepared two answers — one that is polite but kind of wordy, and one that is a little smart-mouthed. To those who are genuinely concerned, I push a button to say, **"I have spastic bilateral quadriplegia, also known as cerebral palsy. It limits my body, but not my mind."** I think that last part is pretty cool.

To people like Claire and Molly, I say, **"We all have disabilities. What's yours?"** I couldn't wait to use that one. When I showed Mrs. V, she laughed so hard, she snorted.

Now it's the Saturday before the tryouts, and Mrs. V and I are sitting outside on her front porch. I'm wearing a light jacket, but it's one of those rare warm February days that fools the hyacinths into thinking spring is here. I want to warn the little buds and say, *Wait! It's gonna snow next week. Stay put for another month!* But every year the early spring flowers shiver in the last snow of the season.

We watch wisps of clouds hover over us. A canary-colored goldfinch is perched on the railing, looking at the empty bird feeder dangling above it. If he could talk, I bet he'd ask for thistle — and more warm days like this.

"What would you do if you could fly?"

Mrs. V asks as she glances from the bird to me.

"Is that on the quiz?" I ask, grinning as I type.

"I think we've studied just about everything else." Mrs. V chuckles.

"I'd be scared to let go," I type.

"Afraid you'd fall?" she asks.

"No. Afraid it would feel so good, I'd just fly away." It took me a long time to type that.

She is quiet for a very long time. Finally, she says, "You *are* a bird, Melody. And you *will* fly on Monday when you take the test."

I hear our front door slam shut next door, and I wave to Mom and Penny as they wander over to the porch. Butterscotch, clearly happy to be unleashed, bounds next to them, sniffing the base of every tree.

Penny walks with such determination, her face alternating between frowns and smiles as she concentrates on marching down the path between our two houses, then climbing the front steps with both hands and both feet. She's wearing her puffy winter jacket and the hat of the day — a blue straw thing that is scrunched and crooked from her sitting on it so many times. Poor Doodle, of course, drags behind her.

"Dee-Dee!" she cries as she finally gets to

the top step. I'm still boggled by how easily she does stuff.

I touch the sleeve of Mrs. V's dress as I think about what she asked me. **"Freedom,"** I type, pointing at Penny. **"Freedom."**

Mrs. Valencia nods. She understands.

"What a glorious day!" Mom says, breathing deeply. "You think we're done with winter?"

"More cold coming," I type.

"You're right, but it sure is a nice preview," Mom says as she unzips Penny's jacket. "How's the study team progressing?"

Butterscotch rests at the bottom of the steps. I swear the dog looks like she's smiling.

"Good," I say through my Medi-Talker.

"Violet, you're amazing," Mom says. "The time and effort you've put into teaching her and getting her ready for this test, and . . ." She breaks off, blinking hard. "You must have taught her *thousands* of words."

"Nobody seems to be amazed that Penny is soaking up and learning thousands of words," Mrs. V replies with a shrug. "Melody is no different."

Mom nods in agreement. "I know you're right, but — but . . . it's just so much *harder* for Melody."

"No, it's harder for *us*. We have to figure out what's in her head."

I'm getting tired of them talking about me like I'm in another room. I turn the volume on my machine up loud. **"Let's have cookies."**

"Cookies!" Penny repeats.

Mrs. V stands up. "I hear you, Penny babe. Let me find us some sweets!" As she heads into the house, she turns to Mom and says softly, "Miz Melody here has always had a special place in my heart."

"Heartburn!" I type.

That gets them both laughing.

Mrs. V returns a few minutes later with a plate of hot chocolate chip cookies and two servings of milk in red sippy cups decorated with Disney princesses. I hate to admit it, but a sippy cup makes it easier for me to drink.

"Cookies!" Penny screams. She reaches for the plate, but Mom pulls her arm back.

Mrs. V gives Mom two cookies on a paper towel. Mom blows on one, then gives it to Penny, who proceeds to stuff the whole thing in her mouth.

"Look at my little Penny pig," Mom says, laughing.

Mrs. V breaks my cookie into segments, then places a piece in my mouth. Although

I'm a caramel lover, these cookies must have been made in chocolate heaven. I swallow while Mrs. V gives me sips of cool milk. Cookies smoosh down so great with milk — I don't even have to try to chew. I'd love to have enough control to feed myself, but that's on my list of things I'd wish for — along with walking, and taking myself to the bathroom, and — oh, yeah — flying.

Interrupting my thoughts, Mrs. V asks, "What continent produces the largest crop of cacao beans, which give us this chocolate?"

"Africa!" I type.

She nods and gives me another sip of milk. "And which state produces the most milk?"

"California," I reply.

"I think you're ready, Melody!" Mrs. V announces.

Mom reaches over and strokes my cheek. "You're going to rock on Monday!"

"Then what?" I type.

"Then you run for president!" Mrs. V interjects.

"Yeah, right," I tap out.

Just then Dad pulls into our driveway. Boy, does our big old car need a trip to the car wash!

"I guess Chuck got off early today," Mom

says, looking pleased. "Maybe we can get an early dinner."

Dad gets out of the car, stretches, and waves at us.

Penny's face lights up. "Daddy!" she calls out. Standing up, she looks at us with a devilish grin.

"Don't you dare!" Mrs. V warns, in her "I mean it" voice.

Penny ignores her. "Go bye-bye in car!"

She *loves* to ride in the car. It doesn't matter where — the store, the post office — as long as she gets to ride in her little car seat in the back. Doesn't make much sense to me — she falls asleep as soon as we turn the first corner.

She hurriedly bumps down a couple of the porch steps, then two more, waiting for a reaction from Mom.

"Penny Marie Brooks, you bring your little buns right back up here!" my mother cries out. When Mom uses all three names, it's serious.

Penny reaches the bottom of the steps, looks back at us, smirks, and says, "See Daddy! Gotta go to work!" Then, as fast as her short little legs will carry her, she bolts for Dad.

Mom, of course, has other ideas. So does Butterscotch, who jumps up, gives three short barks — almost like Mom using three names — and calmly walks in front of Penny to block her path.

"Good dog," Mom says. "Come back here, little cookie face!" By this time she has hurried down the porch steps and retrieved my sister. "This child," she says to my dad, who is ambling over to us, "is an escape artist! I need four sets of eyes with her!" She wipes the chocolate off Penny's face and nuzzles her.

"Good thing you've got Butterscotch," Dad says as he brushes the top of the dog's head. "How's my shiny copper Penny to-day?" Dad kisses Mom on the cheek and takes Penny from her. Penny manages to rub the rest of the chocolate from her hands onto the front of Dad's shirt.

"Just what I always wanted," Dad says as he glances down. "Chocolate-covered clothes!" The napkin Mrs. V passes him only smears it more. Dad just laughs.

"Go work, Daddy?"

"Daddy just got home. Give me a break, kiddo." He hands Penny gently to Mrs. V, then sits with Mom on the porch swing. "And how's my favorite Melody?" he asks me.

"Super," I type on my machine.

"Ready for your competition?"

"Yep!" I tap.

Dad gets up and squats in front of me. "You're going to ace that test and make that quiz team!" I can tell he means it.

I believe in me. And my family does. And Mrs. V.

It's the rest of the world I'm not so sure of.

CHAPTER 20

I was right about the weather today. I hope the little crocus buds have tiny wool blankets because the temperature dipped back down to the thirties, and our classroom was chilly when we rolled in this morning.

The public-address system blared the usual Monday-morning announcements about bake sales and soccer practice. Most of the time nobody in H-5, not even Mrs. Shannon, pays much attention to them. The craziness of our morning usually takes over.

Mrs. Shannon had managed to get us a Wii game system — I don't know how. Willy *loves* the baseball program. I have learned to keep out of his way while he pretends to hit the ball as he watches the screen. Sometimes his swings go wide. "A hit!" he'll cry out with triumph, then he'll try to run the bases in the classroom. Even Freddy can't keep up with him.

I usually sit in a corner with my headphones on, trying to tune it all out.

But today I listened carefully to the bulletin. My heartbeat sped up and I jerked my arms with excitement as I heard the principal say, "All students who wish to try out for the Whiz Kids quiz team, please report to Mr. Dimming's room after school."

I stayed nervous all day. I didn't tell Rose what I planned to do. I thought about it, then decided not to. Suppose she said it was a stupid idea? I didn't think I could take that.

Then I spilled tomato soup all over the front of my blouse at lunchtime. Even though Catherine tried to clean it up, you just can't get red stuff out of a white shirt. I felt like a slob. I wish I had thought of that this morning. I could have *told* Mom to pack a change of clothes for me. It's still hard to remember that I can *say* stuff like that now.

I didn't go out for inclusion classes all day — I wanted to study until the last minute — but as soon as the last bell rings, I grab Catherine's arm. **"Hurry!"** I type. **"To Mr. D's room."**

Even though I am in the electric chair, we set it to manual so she could push me. I am too nervous to drive.

When we arrive at Mr. Dimming's room,

a group of kids from my history class are already there, whispering together and going over note cards. They look up in surprise when Catherine wheels me in.

"Hi, Melody," Rose says. "What are you doing here?" Her voice doesn't sound as friendly as usual.

"Quiz team," I type.

"She can't be on the team," I hear Claire whisper to Jessica, wrinkling up her nose. "She's from the retard room!"

Molly thinks that's really funny. She screeches like a blue jay when she laughs.

I decide to ignore them even though I feel my anger rising. I have to stay focused. Several more students file into the room, from both grades five and six. I don't know the sixth graders very well — they have different recess times. I wonder if they're smarter. They've had more time to learn stuff.

A few kids point at me and whisper. When Mr. Dimming hurries in carrying a stack of papers sealed in plastic, he scans the room to see who's here. He frowns slightly when he sees me, but he sets the test papers on his desk and greets us all.

"Welcome," he says. "I'm so glad that so many of you have chosen to try out for the competition this afternoon. It's going to be challenging as well as fun. Are there any questions before we get started?"

Connor, of course, raises his hand.

"Yes, Connor," Mr. Dimming says with a good-natured sigh.

"Uh, will we get pizza and stuff during practice like last year?"

"Don't you think you need to make the team first?" his friend Rodney yells out.

"Rodney is right. Let's do one thing at a time." Mr. Dimming lifts the stack of test papers from his desk and holds them like a treasure.

"I hold in my hand the official test questions from the national Whiz Kids headquarters in Washington, D.C. I will be reading the questions to you, just as it's done in real competitions, and then —" He stops and stares.

Everyone looks around to see what has interrupted him. It's me.

Mr. Dimming taps the stack of papers for a moment, clears his throat, and addresses Catherine. "You know, I don't think it's appropriate for Melody to be here. This is not a recreational activity just for fun. The purpose of this meeting is to choose our official team."

He isn't even speaking to me. He's looking right over my head at Catherine, as if I were invisible. Now I am really mad.

I turn up the volume on my machine — very loud. **"I am here to take the test."**

Mr. Dimming blinks. "Melody, I don't want your feelings to get injured. The test is very hard."

"I am very smart."

"I just don't want you to be hurt, Melody." He sounds sincere. Sort of.

"I'm tough," I type.

"You go, girl!" Rose suddenly says from the front of the room. A few other kids clap their support.

That makes me feel a little better. Just a little.

Catherine speaks up. "By law, she cannot be excluded. You know that, sir."

"Yes, but —"

"Read the questions to the students just as you had planned. They'll write their answers on notebook paper. Melody will record her answers, then print them out for you."

"How do we know you won't be helping her?" Claire asks.

"Because I won't be in the room," Catherine replies. "Too bad, because *you* might need some help!" Catherine grins at her, but Claire just looks away.

I tell Catherine, **"Go now."** I almost push

her away. **"Thank you."**

"Your mom is coming to pick you up?"

"Yes."

"Good luck, Melody. You're my champ, no matter what, you got that?"

"Got it!" I wave as she leaves the room.

Mr. Dimming shrugs his shoulders and continues with the directions. "There are one hundred quiz questions. I will read each prompt one time and each answer only once. You will have thirty seconds to record each response. Please write only the capital letter: 'A,' 'B,' 'C, 'D,' and sometimes 'E.' Are there any questions?"

Claire's hand shoots up.

"Yes?"

"How do we know Melody doesn't have answers stored in her machine? Us normal people aren't allowed to use computers."

"Why are you so worried about Melody?" Rose answers before Mr. D has a chance to. "Are you scared she'll get a higher score than you?"

"No way!"

"Then be quiet so we can get started."

Mr. D smiles at Rose. "Students, get out two sheets of paper. One to write on. One to cover your answers. We believe in honesty, but an extra sheet of paper can't hurt."

Everyone shuffles to find paper and pens.

196

Then a feeling of quiet expectation falls over the room. Mr. Dimming unseals the official test and opens to the first page.

"Let us begin," he says, his voice suddenly sounding *very* official. "Number one. The capital of Colombia is:

A. Brussels

B. Santiago

C. Bogotá

D. Jakarta."

He pauses while everybody scribbles their answers. I punch in the letter *C*. Good old Mrs. V and her capital quiz cards!

"Number two," Mr. Dimming continues. "Gerontology is the study of:

A. The elderly

B. Gerunds

C. Germs

D. Rocks and jewels."

I punched in the letter *A*. So far, so good.

The test continues for the next thirty minutes or so. He asks questions about atoms and clouds, about fish and mammals, about famous religions and dead presidents. Some of the questions I'm sure of. I guess on a couple. The math questions make me sweat. This is the hardest, most exciting thing I'd ever done.

The very last question is a killer.

"And number one hundred," Mr. D says,

relief in his voice. "The small intestine of an average adult, if stretched out vertically, would measure about how long?

A. Eight to twelve inches

B. One to two feet

C. Five to seven feet

D. Twenty to twenty-three feet."

I punch in the letter *D,* hoping I've guessed right, and breathe a sigh of relief. It was over.

"Pencils down, please," Mr. Dimming tells us. "Make sure your name is on your paper, then cover it with the cover sheet and pass it up to me."

As everyone gathers papers and scribbles their names hurriedly, I push the print button on my Medi-Talker. A slim sheet with my answers emerges from the side. Mr. Dimming walks back to where I sit and rips it off. He doesn't look at me.

"We're done here," he tells the class. "Your parents were told what time to pick you up, but if anyone has a problem with a ride, let me know. I won't leave the building until everyone has safely left school grounds."

I am the last one out. I know my mom will probably come in to get me, but I want to leave on my own power. I turn on my chair and wheel around to face the door.

"Melody," Mr. D calls.

I spin back around.

"I hope you were not discouraged by all this. I was only trying to protect you from being hurt."

"I'm okay," I tell him.

"I'll be announcing the scores and the members of the team tomorrow. I just don't want you to be disappointed."

"I understand." Then I ask him, **"Top eight scores get picked?"**

"Yes. Four team members and four alternates."

I am tired, and I've started to drool a little. I'm sure he thinks I'm a dunce — a sloppy one at that. I feel like the red stain on my blouse is screaming.

"Okay. Good night."

"Good night, Melody. See you tomorrow. And, uh, you might want to wipe your mouth."

I rub the sleeve of my shirt across my lips. The tomato-stained shirt. I can imagine what he was thinking.

I almost bump into my mom as she hurries in.

"How did you do, sweetie?" she asks breathlessly.

"Okay, I guess."

To Mr. D, she says, "Thank you for giving her the opportunity to participate."

"My pleasure, Mrs. Brooks. Melody is a delight, and I'm amazed she's been able to achieve as well as she has."

Yeah, right. A delight with drippy lips and a dirty shirt.

"Let's go, Mom," I type. I need to go to the bathroom, and I want to go home.

CHAPTER 21

Going to the bathroom at school just plain sucks. I have to be taken out of my chair, lifted onto the toilet, and held there so I don't fall. Then someone has to wipe me when I'm finished.

It's not so bad when it's Mom, but it's awful when a classroom aide has to do that for me. She is required by law to wear plastic gloves — I guess in case I have some kind of infection or disease. It's completely embarrassing. I don't usually have to go first thing in the morning, but I'm so nervous on Tuesday, I ask to be taken twice.

Then I go to all my inclusion classes. The students who tried out for the quiz team can't stop chatting about the test. I listen to every word.

"I couldn't believe how easy it was," Connor boasts.

"I bet I got a higher score than you did," Claire says, her voice cocky.

"I thought the geography questions were off the map," Rose adds. "I never even heard of some of those countries."

Jessica shakes her head. "The math part wasn't much fun either."

"I can't believe we even *care* about a dumb test for a quiz team," Rodney comments.

"Because the competition is *on television,* man!" Connor replies. "Big-time TV coverage here in town, and if we make the finals, we go to D.C., where it will be televised all over the country. If we win, we get to be on *Good Morning America.* My grandma in Philly can watch me, and my auntie in Frisco. I'll be famous!"

"What do you mean, *if* we win, Connor?" Claire asks him. "Don't you mean *when* we stomp the competition?"

"Yeah, for sure. I already bought a new suit for when I'm on TV."

Rose rolls her eyes. "I thought this was a team contest, Connor," she reminds him.

"Hey! The team would be nothing without me!" He holds his hand up in the air for high fives.

I listen quietly from the back of the room. When the bell rings to indicate that it's time for Mr. Dimming's class, my palms feel sweaty.

Catherine pushes me into the room and whispers into my ear, "Relax. You rock."

Mr. Dimming gets the class quiet and takes attendance. Why do teachers go so slowly when you want something from them?

Finally, he removes a sheet of paper from his briefcase. "I graded your quiz team tests last night, and since many of those who tried out for the competition team are in this class, I'm going to share the results with you now. The teachers of the other classes who have students who tried out have been given this same list and are at this moment reading the results to them."

"So read the list!" Connor shouts, getting up from his desk.

"If classroom behavior were a determining factor for making the team, Connor, you might be in trouble," Mr. Dimming says. "Please quiet down for a moment."

That shuts him up, and he sits down heavily.

"First of all, I'm very proud of all of you who took the test. It was quite challenging, and you all did extremely well."

Rose raises her hand.

"Yes, Rose?"

"Can we see the questions and answers later so we know where we messed up?"

"Absolutely. As a matter of fact, we'll use this test as a learning tool to study for the real competition. But anyone is free to see the test and check their responses."

"*Please* read the names!" Connor says, as politely as I've ever heard him.

Mr. Dimming smiles. "Okay. Will do. I shall read the alternates first. Two fifth graders. Two from sixth grade. Amanda Firestone. Molly North. Elena Rodriguez. Rodney Mosul."

My heart falls to my shoes, which is not quite to the floor, but close. How could I have missed so many questions? Maybe my thumb slipped and I pushed the wrong letters. Catherine squeezes my hand.

Molly and Rodney screech with joy. Amanda and Elena are sixth graders. Connor is noticeably quiet.

"And now," Mr. Dimming continues, "the names of the four students who scored the highest and will represent our school at the local competition downtown. The alternates will accompany them and will be called upon if any of the team members are unable to participate in any way. Are we ready?"

"Ready," Connor says softly. I notice he has his fingers crossed behind his back.

"I'm proud to report that all four are from

our classroom." He pauses. "To know all the finalists are from fifth grade blows me away. Way to go!"

"We torched grade six? Awesome!" Rodney says. "Now read the names before Connor wets his pants!" Connor reaches over and smacks Rodney on the back of his head.

Mr. Dimming takes a deep breath. "The top four scorers and members of our quiz team will be . . . Connor Bates —"

Connor interrupts him with a wild, whooping cheer. Of course.

"And if I may continue," Mr. D says over his glasses, "we also are pleased to welcome Claire Wilson and Rose Spencer."

Claire's smile is smug.

"But that's only three," Connor says, looking around in confusion.

"I can count, Connor," Mr. Dimming replies dryly.

"So who's the last person on the team?" Molly asks.

Earthquake report: TV weather guys feel some strange activity coming from a local school. Could it be a girl's heartbeat — pounding too hard?

Mr. Dimming clears his throat. "I must apologize. I think we have all underestimated a member of our class."

Earthquake report: This is the big one.

He continues. "In my fifteen years of running this competition I have *never* had a student make a perfect score on the practice test. It is designed to be challenging, to weed out the weaker candidates. In a word, it's hard."

"Tell me about it," Connor mumbles.

"When Melody Brooks took that little practice quiz with us last week, I thought it was a lucky accident that she did so well. But yesterday Melody blew us all away. She got every single question right." He pauses, making sure everyone is taking this in, and then he says, "All of them."

Earthquake report: Walls are tumbling everywhere!

"So she's on the team?" Rose asks, disbelief in her voice.

"Yes, she's on the team."

"But . . . but . . . we'll look weird!" Claire counters. "Everybody will stare at us."

"I'm not going to have any of that kind of talk, do you understand?" Mr. D says sternly. "I'm very proud of Melody. I regret I underestimated her, and I'm glad to have her on our team."

Earthquake report: Call the paramedics. A girl in fifth grade is about to explode.

Everybody in the class turns to look at

206

me. Catherine gives me a hug, Rose flashes me a smile, and I try not to kick and drip and make my teammates sorry that I'll be on the team with them.

"Will the Whiz Kids folks be cool with Melody?" Molly asks.

Mr. Dimming looks thoughtful. "I'll contact the quiz team officials and let them know about our special circumstances," he says. "But that's no concern of yours. Now listen up! Team members will meet every day after school for two hours for the next two weeks — right up until the first competition. Practice sessions are mandatory. Here is paperwork for your parents to read and sign. I need it back tomorrow."

Earthquake report: Expect big aftershocks — nothing like this has ever been seen before.

The more I think about it, the more excited I get. Television! Pressure! People looking at me! I can feel myself getting tense and tight. My arms and legs start doing the tornado spastic dance. My head jerks. I try not to, but I screech — just a little.

Everybody turns at the sound. I can see Molly and Claire jerking their hands, kicking their legs, and making crazy noises. A few people giggle. Mr. Dimming's face grows tight.

I aim all my energy at my thumb and

point to **"Go."**

Catherine gets the message and hurries me out of there.

I want to find a hole and hide in it.

CHAPTER 22

The next two weeks pass in a whirlwind.

In spite of my little display of weirdness that Tuesday in class, I showed up at practice on Wednesday afternoon as if nothing had happened. Maybe nothing had. I was just being me. I'm not sure what the others thought. They said nothing about it.

So, like all the other team members — alternates and regulars alike — I stayed every day after school to practice, from three thirty to almost six o'clock.

I still couldn't get over the fact I was part of the team. Okay. Truth. There was the team, and there was me, and we were in the same room. But we weren't quite a team. They appreciated the fact that I usually got the answers right, but . . .

When Mr. Dimming gave us multiple-choice questions to answer, I had to think for only a moment, then hit the correct letter on my machine. But lots of the preparation involved fast-and-furious, back-and-forth discussions, and I had trouble adding anything to what was being said — most of the time.

"One of the longest one-syllable words in the English language is 'screeched'," Connor announced one afternoon as he chomped on a raspberry Twizzler.

"That's a good word for Melody," Claire said as she snatched his candy and took a bite.

I couldn't respond, and nobody else bothered to.

"What do you call that dot that goes over the letter 'i'?" Elena asked the group.

I knew the answer, but it took me too long to spell out the word.

"It's called a 'tittle,' " Amanda answered quickly. "Like the brain of a fifth grader!"

"Ooh, snap!" said Rodney.

I had planned to type *snap* when she said that too, but I was too slow. The group had already zoomed on to another question.

Gee, they talk fast.

"Who was the first child born in the American colonies?" Rose asked, reading from a huge stack of three-by-five cards in her hand.

"Virginia Dare," Elena answered. "Okay, my turn." She flipped through her own cards — color-coded. "Who was the first Miss America?"

"That's dumb," Connor said. "They're not gonna ask stupid girl stuff like that."

"You don't know the answer?" Claire asked him.

"Of course I know," Connor replied with a snort. "Margaret Gorman. In 1921. She was sixteen and probably looked better than you!" He and Rodney were the only ones to laugh.

Rodney jumped in then. "I've got a nasty question. What is 'pediculosis'?"

Without missing a beat, Rose answered, "When you've got a scalp full of head lice! Yeeww. Do you know that from personal experience?"

"Of course not. I was just looking for a hard word," Rodney told her. He and Connor didn't laugh that time.

"You want a hard word — I've got one," Amanda told the group. "What is 'hexadectylism'?"

That seemed to stump all of them for a minute, so I had time to tap on the number 6, followed by the word *fingers,* then I pushed play so they could all hear my answer.

"Good job, Melody!" Elena said.

"How does she know all this stuff?" Claire

whispered to Rose.

"She's smart!" Rose said, flipping through more cards.

"But she'll look odd on TV, don't you think?" Claire continued, as if I couldn't hear her.

I was ready for her. I had typed a couple of things the night before, so all I had to do was push a button. **"TV makes lots of people look funny,"** I had the machine say. **"Maybe even you, Claire."**

"Ooh, look who's got snaps now!" Connor hooted. "Good one, Melody!"

If I could have danced, I would have!

But as quickly as that moment happened, it disappeared. The team zipped on at rocket-paced speed, feeding off one another's knowledge and skill. At the rate they were going, there was no way I could jump in quick enough. I listened, however, and remembered it all.

"What's the only rock that floats?"

"Pumice."

"How many chromosomes does a human have?"

"Forty-six."

"What was the first state to allow women to vote?"

"Wyoming."

"What's Mr. Dimming's first name?"

"Wallace!"

We all cracked up at that.

At the end of every prep session Mr. Dimming gave us another official quiz from national headquarters. Since those always consisted of multiple-choice questions, I always did well, but I wanted to be like the rest of them as we studied.

One Thursday in the middle of a practice session, Rose's mom ordered pizza for everyone and had it delivered to the school.

"Your mom rocks," Connor said.

"You're easy to please, Connor," Rose replied with a laugh.

Everybody rushed to get the hot, spicy-smelling slices from the box. I was starving like the rest of them, but I just sat there.

"Don't you want some pizza?" Elena asked me. "I'll go get a slice for you." She never said much during the practices, but she took lots of notes and she usually scored pretty high on our practice quizzes.

"Not hungry."

How could I explain to her that without Catherine or my mom or Mrs. V, I wasn't able to eat? I had to be fed like a baby. And I made a mess even then.

When my mom came to pick me up, she asked me if I wanted to stop by Pizza Hut on the way home.

I just shook my head.

CHAPTER 23

The day of the actual competition dawns bright and chilly. I shiver in the early March air as Mrs. V and I wait for my school bus. My jacket feels good. We've decided to use the manual chair today since the electric one, even with the car ramps, is a little too heavy for Mom to handle on her own.

"You ready, Mello Yello?" Mrs. V asks me.

"Oh, yeah!"

"Your head feel like it's gonna pop with all those facts stuck inside?" she teases.

"Oh, yeah!" I grin at her.

"You'll do fine. Better than fine. Dynamite. Possibly awesome!" Mrs. V says.

"Oh, yeah!" I push again.

"We'll all be downtown in the audience cheering you on."

"And the team?"

"There are others on the team?" she asks, smacking herself on her forehead. "I thought you were a solo act!"

215

"And teams from other schools?"

"Don't worry — you're smarter than all of them put together! So we'll be cheering the loudest — your mom and dad and me and Penny."

"Do I look okay?"

Mrs. V looks me up and down. "Like a television star!" she replies. "Your mom tucked an extra blouse in your bag, just in case. Catherine knows what to do."

I'm glad Catherine will be going with us, and I think Mr. Dimming is glad as well.

"Tell me the plan again."

"Your mom will pick you up from school, take you to get a bite to eat, and get you to the TV studio about fifteen minutes before the rest of the contestants. Penny and your dad and I will meet you there."

"TV folks won't freak out when I show up?"

"They are well prepared for you. Actually, it's possible a few reporters might be there and want to talk to you."

"Me? Why?" I can't imagine why any newsperson would want to talk to somebody who can only talk through a machine. How boring.

"You're a wonderful human-interest story. Other people might be interested in knowing more about you."

216

"They won't make fun of me?" Just the thought of it makes my palms sweaty.

Mrs. V takes my hand in hers. "Not at all. They'll admire you, I'm sure. You are Spaulding Street Elementary School's own personal Stephen Hawking. They're lucky!"

"Hope so."

"Here's your bus. Have a great day, Melody. I'll see you tonight."

I manage to get through the day without spilling anything on my clothes, and I'm relieved to see Mom when the last bell rings at school. After a quick meal of macaroni and applesauce in the car — smart Mom, nothing red — we head downtown.

We find a handicapped parking spot right in front of the studio, and after the usual unloading the chair down the car ramps, seating me and strapping me in, then attaching Elvira, we roll inside. The receptionist, a chunky, pleasant woman with lots of makeup and frizzy hair, directs us to the staging area.

I have to blink a little to figure it all out. Everything you see on TV is fake. I see the place where they film the news. When I watch it on television at home, it looks like the reporters are sitting in front of a huge window that shows all of downtown. But it's just a painting, and it's pretty small. So is the desk where the reporters sit. It seems so much bigger from home.

I recognize a couple of the reporters who I watch every day. I can't believe how *skinny* the morning lady is. On TV she looks normal-size. I'm going to look like a huge balloon when the cameras show me.

Speaking of cameras, *they* are huge — like giant, black mechanical space beings on wheels. Guys with headphones and women with clipboards run around checking stuff. The back part of the studio is dark, but the place where the contest will take place is lit brightly. I can see where the teams will stand and the big buttons they'll push for the answers.

In another room, behind all the cameras and the action, are the benches where the audience sits. Some people have already started to file in. I can see them through a large glass window.

I jump when Catherine taps me on the shoulder. "Fascinating, huh?"

"For real," I type.

She and Mom chat a bit before a man wearing jeans and a Cincinnati Bengals sweatshirt approaches us. "Excuse me," he says to me, "but are you Melody Brooks?"

Surprised, I quickly hit **"Yes."**

"My name is Paul, and I'm the stage

218

manager." His huge hand swallows mine as he shakes it. "I'm glad you're here early. Let's see if we have you set up correctly. We're really glad to have you participate."

He spoke directly to me, not Mom or Catherine! I like him right away.

We roll across the studio, careful to avoid cords and wires, and enter the area where the competition will take place.

"This is where the members of each team will stand," he explains. "They each have four large buttons to push. Red is for the letter 'A.' Blue is for the letter 'B.' Yellow is for the letter 'C.' And 'D,' of course, is green."

I nod.

"And here, Miss Melody, is where *you* will sit. Right next to your teammates. I have rigged a special answer board for you, so it's adjusted to the height of your wheelchair." He looks pretty proud of himself as he shows me the setup.

"Wow!" I type. **"This is perfect. How did you know?"**

"My son is in a wheelchair," he says with a shrug. "I build stuff for Rusty all the time, but there's no way he could do what you are about to do." He kneels down so he can look me in the eye. "Knock their socks off, champ! Rusty will be watching."

"Okay!" I type. **"For Rusty."**

He rolls me behind my answer board and lets me practice with the four color-coded buttons. Because they are so large, hitting the right one is actually easier than using my Medi-Talker. I don't even have to aim with my thumb — I can use my whole fist.

When I hit the red button, the letter *A* lights up on the screen in front of me to lock in the answer.

"Thanks, Paul," I type. **"Very, very much."**

He winks, gives all of the buttons a quick punch to make sure they all light up, then tells me he'll see me later.

"I can do this," I tell Mom and Catherine. **"I'm ready."**

The rest of our team starts to arrive. Connor, dressed in a black suit with a red tie, actually looks good. Rose, blushing and nervous, is wearing pale blue.

"Hi, Melody," she says. "Are you scared?

"Nope! Not at all," I type.

"My mom made me wear this tie," Connor complains as he rolls his finger inside his shirt collar to loosen it. "I hope I don't choke on live TV!"

If he does, at least the attention will be on him instead of me. What if I do something stupid or I start to drool and the camera

220

does a close-up?

Amanda, Rodney, Molly, and Elena — the alternates — look a little sad as they wander around the studio. They won't get a chance to participate unless something happens to disqualify one of the four of us. I guess that includes Connor fainting or me convulsing.

"Are you okay?" I hear Rose ask Amanda.

"Yeah. But it's just like I'm all dressed up with nothing to do."

"I feel you," Rose says.

"Break a leg," Amanda tells her.

"Really?" Rose smiles.

"That's what you're supposed to say for good luck," Amanda explains.

"I know. But look at it this way. At the finals in Washington, there are six people on the team. So that opens things up a little."

"So go out there and win!"

"Will do!"

Claire and Molly make funny faces in front of the cameras, pretending they are on the air. Neither speaks to me.

"Look, Claire!" Molly says, her voice, for once, in awe of something. "You can see your reflection in that camera over there!"

"Do I look okay?" Claire asks, smoothing her dress.

"You look great," Molly assures her.

"You know, it really ought to be *you* up

there instead of Melody," Claire says loud enough for me to hear.

"Well, I'm ready if she messes up," Molly whispers back.

I just shake my head and think, *Delete, delete, delete.* No way am I letting their negativity mess me up. I have enough to worry about.

Mr. Dimming hurries in then, wearing a brand-new navy blue suit, a fresh white shirt, and a red vest and tie. The whole team cheers, and Connor gives him a high five.

He buzzes around for a bit, like a nervous bumblebee. He checks on details, wishes us all good luck, then goes to sit in the observation area. No teachers are allowed near the students during the competition. Catherine is allowed to stand in the back behind the cameras, just in case I have an emergency.

Other teams start to fill the studio as well. One team, from Green Hills Academy, is all dressed in Kelly green sweaters. Not a bad idea, but the sweaters are ugly.

Another team, from Crown Elementary, is wearing little fake crowns on their heads. That seems to me a little over the top.

Our team hasn't done anything special. They don't need to. They have me.

Chapter 24

It's time.

"Cameras rolling!" someone calls out. "In five, four, three, two . . ." He points at the man at center stage.

The moderator, a slim guy with hair that looks like it has been glued into place, brushes a speck off his tuxedo, adjusts his red-striped tie, and begins speaking right on cue. "Good evening!" he says with that perfectly modulated voice that announcers seem to be born with. "My name is Charles Kingsley, and I'd like to welcome you to the Whiz Kids Southwest Ohio Regional Competition!"

Cheers all around.

"In two weeks the winner of this competition will travel to Washington, D.C., to represent our area at the national championships."

More cheers.

"We wish the best of luck to all our young

competitors!"

The studio quiets.

"The rules are simple," Mr. Kingsley explains. "Teams will be asked twenty-five questions. Each correct answer from each four-member team is worth one point, so the maximum total team score is one hundred points."

He pauses so the cameras can show the scoreboard.

Then he announces, "The two teams with the *highest* scores from all preliminary rounds will meet for what we call a 'quiz-off,' so point totals are critical. The winner of that final set of quiz questions will be declared our local elementary-school-level champion and will proceed to the nationals in Washington. The team that emerges as the winner will appear live on national television on *Good Morning America* the next morning!"

Cheers and applause.

"Our first two teams to compete tonight will be Woodland Elementary and Spaulding Street Elementary. Take your places, ladies and gentlemen."

The four contestants from Woodland and the other three members of our team walk to the testing area, waving for the cameras. Catherine rolls me to my position, makes sure I can easily reach the buttons, then she gives me a quick hug and walks away.

"I'd like to take a moment," Mr. Kingsley says, "to introduce a very special participant in our competition tonight. Her name is Melody Brooks."

The cameras all point in my direction. The studio lights are incredibly bright — and hot. I blink rapidly. I feel damp and sweaty.

"Although the other contestants will stand, Melody will be seated as she answers the questions. We've made adjustments to our answer board so that she can access the buttons, but nothing else. I hear she's a fierce competitor."

I try to wave, but I figure I look goofy and wobbly, so I pull my hand down.

Rose stands next to me, with Connor in the middle and Claire on the far end.

"I feel like I'm gonna throw up," I hear Claire whisper.

"Don't you dare!" Connor hisses.

"We'll start with a practice round, so you can familiarize yourself with our button system. Everyone ready? Which of the following is a mammal?

A. Cat
B. Bird
C. Turtle
D. Spider."

Everybody, including me, pushes *A,* of course. The screens in front of us light up with the letter *A.*

"Don't you wish all the questions would be that easy?" Mr. Kingsley asks, chuckling.

Yeah, right.

"Remember two things," he reminds everyone. "First, this is a *team* competition, and second, this is not a test of speed, but of accuracy. Teams get more points if all four contestants come up with the correct answer. And the two teams with the most points meet for the finals. Are we ready?"

"Ready!" the seven contestants on stage answer.

I start to hit the word *ready* on my board, but I decide to concentrate on the contest instead.

"Round one will have twenty-five questions. Let us begin. Number one."

I tense. *Here we go!*

"The average lifespan of an adult mayfly can range from:

A. One minute to one hour

B. Thirty minutes to one day

C. One day to one week

D. Two weeks to one month."

Bing! Bing! Bing! Bing! Everyone hits their buttons. Once the answers are locked in, the readouts are displayed. Everyone on our team answered *B*. One person on the Woodland team answered *A*.

Mr. Kingsley smiles and says, "Woodland has three points and Spaulding now has four with all correct responses."

We can do this. I can do this. Bring on the next one!

"Number two," he intones. "The battles of Lexington and Concord in the American Revolutionary War were fought in what year?

A. 1774

B. 1775

C. 1776

D. 1777."

That one is a little tricky. I press *B*, however. So does everyone else. The score is now seven to eight.

Mr. Kingsley continues. "In literature the word 'oxymoron' means which of the following?

A. A combination of contradictory words

B. The outcome of a sequence of events

C. An implied reference to a literary or historical event

D. A symbolic story or narrative."

I am fairly sure the answer is *A*, but that word could mean "big-headed crippled kid who thinks she can win in a national quiz competition."

When the answer is shown on the screen,

Connor got it wrong, and so did two members of the Woodland team. So the score is now set at Woodland: nine, Spaulding: eleven. We're still up, but we have twenty-two more questions to go.

"The next question," Mr. Kingsley says, "deals with math."

Oh, crap. I'm dead meat.

"There are two thousand three hundred fifty-seven paintings in an art museum. The museum has one hundred twenty-four rooms. Which is the reasonable estimate for the number of paintings in each room?

A. 10

B. 20

C. 60

D. 200."

Yep. Dead, rotten meat. Let's see — I've got to visualize a museum . . . and rooms . . . and lovely paintings. How many in a room? Not sure. Divide what into what? Not sure. I'm going to say sixty.

When the answer flashes as *B,* I feel like an idiot. But Rose got it wrong too, and so did two kids on the Woodland team. The score stands at thirteen to eleven.

By the time we get to the twenty-fifth question, I'm sweaty and thirsty, but I'm pumped. The lead bounced back and forth between the two teams a couple of times.

Sometimes they were in front of us, and sometimes we forged ahead with points. I got most of the language arts answers right, but the math questions stumped me.

Connor can't spell, so he missed several of those questions. Rose is weak in history. Claire has trouble with science. The Woodland team was about the same — some kids good in some areas, others good in others.

"We now come to the final question for our first two teams," Mr. Kingsley announces. He clears his throat and begins: "A weather event that measured 6.5 on the Richter scale would be a/an:

A. Tornado
B. Hurricane
C. Earthquake
D. Tsunami."

Bing! Bing! Bing! Bing!

I punch *C* and relax. I did not have a tornado spaz. Connor, Rose, and Claire all got the final question correct as well. Two people on the Woodland team answered "hurricane" instead. When the results are tallied, our team has a total of eighty-one points. Woodland ends up with seventy-seven.

"Congratulations, Spaulding!" Mr. Kingsley says with a polished smile. "The two highest-scoring teams will meet for the final round later tonight. Good luck, and we hope we see you again."

Victory! For round one.

As the show breaks for a commercial, we are all escorted to a special waiting room in the back. The students from Woodland look really disappointed. That's it for them for the whole competition. All they can do now is watch as the second two teams head to the stage for their session under the lights.

Mom, Dad, Penny, Mrs. V, and Catherine are all waiting for me in the back room, hugging me and kissing me like I've won the lottery or something. Catherine does a little happy dance. Dad tells me he filmed the whole thing on his camcorder.

"You rocked, Melody!" Mrs. V shouts.

"I am sooooo proud of you, sweetie!" my mom says.

"Can I have a Coke?" I type as quickly as I can. I feel breathless.

Everybody laughs as Catherine rushes to find me a paper cup for the sodas that are sitting on ice in the waiting room for the contestants.

Mom pours dribbles of the ice-cold Coke into my mouth, one sip at a time, making sure I don't spill on my shirt. I am *so* thirsty, I don't even care that people from the other teams are staring at me.

230

Mr. Dimming, after talking to Rose and Connor and Claire, bounds over to us, beaming. "This is such a thrill, Melody! You were amazing out there! I'm so proud of our team and extremely proud of you."

"Thanks," I tap. **"What's next?"**

"We wait for the next teams to compete, then we'll meet and beat the other high-scoring team and pack our bags for Washington!"

"Don't pack yet," I type with a grin on my face.

"I've been packed for ten years," he tells me. "I've just been waiting for the right team. This is our year. I just know it."

He wanders off to talk to other parents. I never thought about what teachers dream about. I had no idea what a big deal this is for him.

Rose comes over and squats down next to Penny. "I like your hat," she tells Penny, who is holding Doodle closely and wearing a blue polka-dotted hat with a red feather.

"Wo-sie!" Penny says gleefully.

"How's my favorite baby girl?" Rose says in her whispery voice.

"Wo-sie!" Penny repeats.

"You did really good, Melody," Rose says to me.

"You too," I type.

"You think we have a chance for the finals?"

"Yep!"

"And Washington?"

"Yep!"

"And being on *Good Morning America*?"

"Oh, yeah!"

Claire stays on the other side of the room with her parents, but Connor ambles over and stands next to Rose.

"You're okay, Melody," he says. "You beat me on a couple of those!"

"You rock in math," I tell him.

"I know," he replies with a grin, "but I still can't spell! I hope they don't have any spelling questions in the finals."

"I gotta go to the bathroom!" Rose says suddenly. "I am *so* nervous about the finals!" She hurries out. I know what she means. Butterflies. Moths. Giant bumblebees flutter inside me.

When *we* were on camera, it felt like it took a million years to complete our round, but in just a few minutes the second set of contestants come back to the waiting room. The school with the little crowns won round two with seventy-nine points. Then, within another half hour, Edison Elementary clinches the third round with a score of eighty.

Finally, a school called Perry Valley wins the fourth round with eighty-two points, just one point more than us.

"I watched them," Mrs. V tells me when they troop back into the room, excited and victorious. "They're really good."

"Should we worry?" I ask.

"Of course not! Our team is the best because they have a secret weapon — you!"

Suddenly, there is a rush of activity in the room as stagehands come in to get us. "Perry Valley and Spaulding Street, we need you back on camera for the finals! You are our two top-scoring schools. Congratulations!"

We hurry back to our places.

The lights seem brighter this time.

Mr. Kingsley returns to his position, gets his microphone adjusted by the stage crew, and shouts, "Welcome back, ladies and gentlemen, to the final round of our regional Whiz Kids competition! The winners of this round will represent us all in Washington, D.C., in just two weeks! All members of the winning team, along with their chaperones, will receive an all-expenses-paid trip to our nation's capital, three nights in a hotel, and tours of the city."

"Trophy! Trophy!" someone yells.

"Oh, the famous Whiz Kids Championship award! The winning team in Washington gets to take home that *huge* golden trophy, they receive a guest appearance on *Good Morning America,* and their school will receive a check for two thousand dollars to be used for academic endeavors!"

Lots of whoops at that.

"Let us begin. Teams, are you ready?"

"Ready!" they all reply.

I am ready too.

CHAPTER 25

OMG! What a night! I still can't believe how everything turned out once the championship round began. That's when Mr. Kingsley explained, "The questions this time will be a bit more difficult. Scoring, however, will be the same. The team with the best score out of one hundred possible points will be our champion."

He picked up the cards that contained the quiz questions and smiled. "Here is question number one. What is 'diplopia'?

A. Double vision

B. Left-handedness

C. A disease of the gums

D. A form of cancer."

Oh, boy! He wasn't kidding! This was going to be a killer round. I was sure the answer was *A,* though. Kind of.

When the answer was revealed, "double vision" was correct.

Whew!

Rose, Connor, and I got it right. Claire missed it. Everyone on the Perry Valley team answered it correctly. The score was three to four.

"Number two," Mr. Kingsley said. "Who is the composer of *Rhapsody in Blue?*

A. Mozart

B. Gershwin

C. Copeland

D. Beethoven."

Bing! Bing! Bing! Bing!

Thanks to my parents and Mrs. V, that was a little easier. I pushed the button for *B.* One person on the Perry Valley team got it wrong, and Claire messed up as well. That made the score six to seven, with Perry Valley ahead. Everybody could feel the tension.

The next twenty questions covered things like lions in the jungle, gravity in space, authors of famous books, and math. Some of those I even got right.

Bing! Bing! Bing! Bing!

Even though Connor aced a hard spelling problem and Claire came through on a difficult history question, Perry Valley kept staying one or two points ahead of us.

It was getting near the end of the round. Perry Valley had surged ahead on a math question and was up by three points. It looked pretty grim for us, with a score of seventy-eight to eighty-one. I glanced at Connor. Sweat dripped from his nose.

Then Mr. Kingsley asked, "The condition in which a person may be able to hear colors or visualize flavors when music is played is called:

A. Synthesis

B. Symbiosis

C. Synesthesia

D. Symbolism."

I grinned and punched in *C*. Not only was it one of Mrs. V's vocabulary words, it was me!

I breathed a sigh of relief when I realized that Connor and Claire and Rose had also chosen the right answer. When the results were tallied, only one of the Perry Valley kids had gotten it right.

The score stood at eighty-two to eighty-two. It was time for the very last question. This one would determine the group that would go to Washington. I glanced at Rose and the others. I think we all gulped at the same time.

"Our last question of the evening," Mr. Kingsley began, "is a mathematics problem."

I groaned inside. *There goes our trip to Washington! I may as well go back to room*

H-5 and hide there for the next thousand years.

"Number twenty-five," Mr. Kingsley said slowly. "Lisa gets up every morning and gets ready for school. She takes twenty-two minutes to get dressed, eighteen minutes to eat breakfast, and ten minutes to walk to school. What time should Lisa get up so she can arrive at school at 7:25 a.m.?

A. 6:15 a.m.
B. 6:20 a.m.
C. 6:25 a.m.
D. 6:35 a.m."

I need to add, then subtract. How do I subtract time? I need to see a clock! I'm getting all mixed up! Time is running out! I can't mess up now!

It could have been *C,* but it might have been *D.* I thought a moment more, then I pushed *D,* feeling like I was going to throw up. The answers lit up on the screen. Everybody on our team had answered *D.* Either we were all correct or all really terrible at figuring out time problems. Three students on the Perry Valley team had answered *D.* One of them had answered *C.*

"Well, it looks like we have a winner, ladies and gentlemen! I'm extremely pleased to announce that the team that will represent us in Washington, D.C., this year, the team we hope to see on *Good Morning America,* with a score of eighty-six to eighty-five, is . . ." He paused for effect. "Spaulding Street Elementary School!"

I couldn't help it. I squealed. I kicked. My arms jerked crazily. I tried *really* hard to control it, but I just couldn't help it. My body went a little wacko on me.

"Shut her up!" I heard Claire hiss.

"Shhh," Rose whispered through clenched teeth.

"Thank you for watching our telecast," Mr. Kingsley said, throwing a quick glance at me. "Please join us in two weeks when we televise the finals from Washington. This is Charles Kingsley, good night."

He signaled that he was finished, the cameras blinked to dark, and the lights, blessedly, clicked off.

I couldn't stop kicking. My arms acted like windup toys gone bananas. I screamed with joy. At least nobody noticed this time, because hoots and hollers abounded as dozens of people stormed the stage.

Dad balanced Penny in one arm and the camcorder in another. Mom, Catherine, and Mrs. V rushed over to me and almost smothered me with hugs. Mrs. V tried to look as if she weren't surprised, but her grin seemed to be permanently attached.

Mr. Dimming, the alternates, and all the parents of the rest of the kids on the team cheered and jumped and patted one another on the back. One of the parents streamed confetti over us. Balloons appeared from nowhere. Somebody in the studio turned the speakers up loud and played the song "Celebration." People started to dance.

It seemed as if a million pictures were taken. Amazingly, lots were being taken of me. I did my best to calm down and relax.

"Smile, Melody!" called a guy with a baseball cap.

Click! Flash!

"Can somebody sit her up a little straighter in her chair?"

Click! Flash!

"Get a picture of the kid in the wheel-chair!" I think that guy was a reporter.

Click! Flash!

"Where's the winning team?" another reporter asked loudly. "We want a team picture for the newspaper! Why don't you kids stand around Melody? Okay now, smile!"

Click! Flash!

I could barely see. Blue dots danced in front of my eyes.

"We want the winning team for a TV interview!" someone else called out. "Can we have them over here?"

People were shuffled around, and a stage-hand helped set us up. Connor, Rose, and Claire sat in chairs next to me. Amanda, Molly, Elena, and Rodney stood behind us. Mr. Dimming stood next to Rodney.

I hoped that my hair looked okay and that I wouldn't look too goofy.

The reporter silenced the crowd as the cameraman lined up and got into position.

"Good evening. This is Elizabeth Ochoa of Channel Six News. I'm here in our studio as we speak to students from Spaulding Street Elementary School, victorious members of the winning team of the Whiz Kids competition held here tonight. These are eight of the brightest young people in our community, who buzzed their way to victory tonight. Let's meet them. We'll start with the alternates in the back row, the youngsters who will fill in should one of the team members not be able to participate. Please tell me your names and ages," she asked as she put the microphone in front of each student.

"Amanda Firestone, age twelve."

"Molly North, age eleven."

"Elena Rodriguez, age twelve."

"Rodney Mosul, age eleven and a half."

That got a laugh.

Ms. Ochoa continued. "And seated in front of me is the championship team! Please tell me your names as well."

"My name is Claire Wilson, and I'm eleven, and I got more right than anyone else on my team."

"Good for you!" Ms. Ochoa said. "I know you studied hard for this." The reporter moved quickly to Rose. "And you are . . . ?"

"Rose Spencer, age eleven," Rose said, sounding shy.

"What stands out for you this evening?" the reporter asked as the camera moved in closer.

"I was on last year's team, and we lost by only a few points, so it's real exciting to win this time. I'm very proud of our team." Rose was beaming.

"Great answer! And we're proud of you as well," Ms. Ochoa said. "And now to this tall young man. Your name, sir?" she asked Connor.

"Connor Bates. Hi, Mom!" Connor spoke loudly into the mike.

"Do you remember the hardest question you were given tonight?" the reporter asked him.

"I thought all the questions were super easy," Connor said with a grin. "I missed a few on purpose so the other contestants

242

wouldn't feel bad!"

Ms. Ochoa burst into a tinkly laugh. "How does it feel to be on a team with your very special team member?" she asked.

"Hey. Melody is okay. She's really smart. Let me introduce you to —"

But I wasn't about to let him steal my thunder. **"My name is Melody Brooks, and I'm eleven years old,"** my machine said loudly and clearly.

The reporter looked amazed. "Well, this is astounding! How does it feel to be part of the winning team, Melody?"

I pressed my key for **"Super."**

She laughed. "Was it difficult to study and prepare for the competition?" Ms. Ochoa asked.

"No. Lots of people helped me."

"What was the hardest part about partici- pating tonight?"

"Hoping I wouldn't mess up!"

She smiled. "We all feel like that some- times. Are you excited about traveling to Washington, D.C.?"

"Oh, yes!"

"Have you ever been there before?"

"No."

"How will being on the winning team change your life at school?"

I thought that was a good question.

"Not much," I admitted. Then the reporter waited patiently while I took the time to tap the right words. **"Maybe kids will talk to me more."**

"I talk to her all the time," Claire interjected.

Both Rose and Connor looked at her with frowns. "Huh?" Rose said.

Ms. Ochoa moved away from me and over to Claire. "So, you consider yourself to be Melody's friend?"

"Oh, absolutely," Claire said with a bounce of her cinnamon-colored curls. "She and I eat lunch together every day and test each other on questions for the quiz team. Melody is a lot smarter than she looks."

Rose raised her hand to speak, but the reporter shook her head. "I'm so sorry, but we're out of time," she told Rose. To the camera, she said, "In addition to a great group of kids, we've just met two remarkable young women — best friends in spite of their differences and members of the winning, Washington-bound Whiz Kids quiz team. Congratulations to you all!"

I was stunned. Claire?

CHAPTER 26

In the midst of all the commotion Mr. Dimming seemed to get an inspiration. "Let's go out to dinner to celebrate!" he announced as the last of the studio lights were turned off.

"Great idea!" Connor said immediately.

"I'm starving!" said Amanda. "Even though I wasn't on camera, I've been too nervous to eat all day."

"Me too!" Elena added.

"How about Linguini's?" Connor suggested. "They've got all-you-can-eat spaghetti." Leave it to Connor to know all the best places to eat.

"They might go out of business after you show up, Connor," Mr. Dimming said with a laugh. "Don't go embarrassing me, now."

"Don't worry, Mr. D. My max is about twelve bowls of spaghetti."

"Linguini's is perfect," Rose's dad said. "It's walking distance — just around the corner from the studio. These kids deserve a special night out!"

I looked at Mom, not sure if this was a good idea.

Then Elena walked over to me and said, "You'll come too, won't you, Melody?"

"Yeah, Melody," Rose added, "come with us. You did really great tonight."

"We couldn't have won without you," Connor said as he buttoned up his coat.

Their words made me feel like one of the helium balloons that some families had brought.

"Well, I wouldn't go that far," Molly said, glancing at Claire.

Balloons do pop.

"*You* weren't up there," Connor reminded Molly.

"So, you comin' or not?" Rose asked.

"Sure," I tapped. **"It will be fun."** I glanced at Mom again, who nodded. Dad took Penny home, and Mrs. V gave me a hug and promised she'd see me in the morning.

The air was brisk and the conversation silly as we headed for the restaurant.

"How many windows do you think are in that office building?" Connor shouted, pointing to the tallest one we could see.

"Five thousand two hundred and seventy-four," Rose answered.

"Man, you're good!" Rodney said. "How did you know that?"

"How do you think I got on the quiz team?" Rose told him. "I've got smarts!"

"She's just guessing," Molly told Rodney. "You believe anything."

The restaurant had been in that location for years. The outside entrance was designed to look like a bistro from a small Italian village. Painted grape leaves and tiny white lights decorated the bricks around the door.

The door.

When Connor's dad opened it for everyone to enter, Connor and Rodney bounded up the steps.

The steps.

Five stone steps led upstairs to the dining area. Everyone, including Mr. Dimming, rushed past me and Mom. Finally, Connor's dad, the last to go up, looked at me, looked at the stairs, and the lightbulb came on.

"Uh, do you need some help?" he asked. He was large, like his son. I bet he could swallow a few bowls of pasta as well.

Mom replied, "Would you be so kind as to ask an employee where their wheelchair ramp is located?"

As if glad to have something to do, Mr. Bates dashed up the steps. Mom and I sat there in the cold. Alone.

A waiter dressed in black rushed down moments later. "I'm so sorry. We have an elevator in the back, but it went on the fritz this afternoon. The technician is coming to fix it first thing in the morning."

"That's not going to help us tonight, is it?" Mom told him. Her voice was tight but not angry.

"I'd be glad to help you carry her up the steps," he offered.

"**No,**" I tapped. My eyes begged Mom.

Mom told him, "Just hold the door for us, young man. We'll be fine."

He did just that. Mom turned her back to the stairs, got a good grip on my chair, tilted it back slightly, and took a deep breath. I was so glad we had decided on the manual chair this morning.

Mom gently rolled the back wheels up the edge of the first stone step.

Pull. Roll up. Bump. First step.

Pull. Roll up. Bump. Second step.

Pull. Roll up. Bump. Third step.

She paused and took another breath. We'd done this before. Many times.

Pull. Roll up. Bump. Fourth step.

Pull. Roll up. Bump. Fifth step.

Then we finally rolled into the dining room, which was crowded with noisy, laughing customers.

"Over here, Melody!" Mr. Dimming called as he saw us.

Mom led me over to our very large table, and I was relieved to see that the group had left a spot for me. With all the kids on the team plus their parents, we took up a big chunk of the table space in the place.

In some restaurants the tables are too low for my chair, but this time I was able to slide perfectly into place. Mom helped me take off my coat, then sat in the seat next to me. She gulped the water from her glass and asked for a refill.

The waitress began to take orders.

Rodney and his parents ordered a large mushroom and onion pizza. "We're vegetarians," Rodney explained. I had no idea.

"Can I get a steak, Dad?" Connor asked.

His dad clapped him on the back. "Sure, I think I'll have one myself. For this one night, you get anything you want!"

Connor's eyes got large. "A whole chocolate cake?"

"You'll barf, boy," his dad replied.

"I want the pasta delight," Rose told the waitress. "With extra cheese."

"Me too!" said Amanda.

"May I have the spaghetti and meatballs, please?" Elena asked.

Claire and Molly both ordered lasagna.

When the waitress got to me and Mom, I was ready.

"I'll have mac and cheese, please," I made Elvira say.

The waitress looked a little surprised, since most of the machine was tucked under the table, but she was cool and acted as if she got orders from Medi-Talkers every day. "Sure, hon. Comin' right up. You want some salad with that?"

"No, thanks."

She gave me a real big smile, then took Mom's order. Only my mom would order baked fish at an Italian restaurant!

As we waited for our food, the cheerful mood continued. Our tables were covered with white paper instead of tablecloths, so everybody, including the adults, had been given crayons and markers.

"Look at this — I drew a giant monster rabbit!" Connor said. He glanced at Rose's drawing, then added large green teeth to his own. "And it's gonna eat that wimpy bug you just drew," he told her.

Rose laughed. "Well, this is a poisonous spider, and it's gonna bite your silly old rabbit!"

Rodney and Connor then lined up all the salt and pepper shakers and started tossing sugar packets over the barricade with forks and spoons as catapults.

But I noticed that Claire, who was sitting next to Rodney, was strangely quiet and didn't even pick up a crayon.

"Engage the enemy!" Connor cried. "Score!"

"You weren't even in my territory, man! Besides, you tossed the pink fake sugar stuff. You only get half a point for that stuff!"

I sat and watched my teammates do such ordinary things. Drawing. Laughing. Teasing. Joking. I really tried hard to look like I was having fun too, but all I wanted to do was go home.

When the waitress finally brought the food, forks became important for eating and the war ended suddenly. Conversation slowed down as everybody dug into their meals. Connor took a huge bite of his steak.

"Mmm, this is the bomb," he said with his mouth full.

Mom's fish looked a little, well, fishy, as she picked at it with her fork. She and I were thinking the same thing, I knew.

My food sat untouched in front of me.

Our family goes out to restaurants every once in a while. Actually, Penny is more of a problem in a restaurant than I am because she's wiggly and excitable and she's likely to throw her peas on the floor.

Usually, eating out doesn't bother me. Mom and Dad take turns spooning food into my mouth, and I ignore anyone who is rude enough to stare.

But this was different. At school I eat in a special area of the cafeteria with the other disabled kids. The aides put bibs on us, feed us, and wipe our mouths when we're done. With the exception of that sip of Coke at the competition, nobody on the team had ever really seen me eat. Rather, be fed.

I didn't know what to do. My food sat there getting cold. I looked at Mom. She looked at me. She picked up the spoon and looked at me with the question on her face.

I nodded. Very carefully, she placed a spoonful of pasta in my mouth. I swallowed. I did not spill.

I saw Molly poke Claire, and they exchanged looks.

Mom spooned one more portion into my mouth. I swallowed. I did not spill. We continued, one spoonful at a time.

I was *so* hungry.

Nobody said anything, but I saw them look down at their plates with way too much attention. It got quiet. Even Connor stopped talking.

Finally, even though my plate was still full,

I pushed it away.

"Would you like to take this home, Melody?" Mom whispered.

I nodded yes, hugely relieved, and she signaled for the waitress, who also brought dessert menus.

Being reminded of cake and ice cream cheered up Connor, who did not order a whole chocolate cake, but did order two slices. Rodney ordered apple pie, while Rose asked for pudding.

Claire ended up taking her food home in a box as well. She had eaten almost nothing and barely said two words all evening.

"So, what did you think about that final question? That was *too* hard!" Rodney said.

"Piece of cake!" Connor replied, laughing at his own joke. He smeared whipped cream over his second piece of cake.

"Did you see the *hair* on that announcer?" Amanda teased. "It never moved!"

"Must have been made of plastic," Rose said, laughing.

"What are you wearing to the D.C. competition?" Rose asked Claire.

Claire just shrugged.

"I wonder if we'll get to visit the White House while we're there," Amanda mused. "That would be awesome."

"I believe it's on our agenda for Saturday,"

Mr. Dimming replied enthusiastically. "I'm excited about that as well!"

"So, what's with you and Melody being best friends, Claire?" Elena asked.

Claire didn't answer, but she rubbed her hand over her forehead. "I don't feel so good," she said weakly. "Is it hot in here?" No one had time to answer, for at that moment Claire stood up suddenly, clamped her hand over her mouth, and stumbled from her seat.

"Are you okay?" Mr. Dimming asked.

Before he could finish the question, Claire threw up all over his new shoes.

"Ooh, gross!" Connor said, obviously trying not to laugh.

"Poor thing," Rose said.

"Whoa, what a stink, man!" Rodney covered his nose.

Claire's mom rushed her to the bathroom.

Mr. Dimming rushed out as well, I guess to clean off his shoes.

I wondered if Claire felt as embarrassed as I had while Mom was feeding me.

Our little victory celebration was clearly over. Parents gathered coats and checks and paid their tabs. Claire returned from the restroom looking pale. No one mentioned the incident. We all headed for the steps.

Hmmm, I thought. *Claire gets sick in the*

middle of a crowded restaurant, yet I'm the one everybody looks at sideways.

They all had to wait for me and Mom. We took our time.

Push gently. Roll down. Bump. Top step.

Push gently. Roll down. Bump. Next step.

Push gently. Roll down. Bump. Third step.

Five bumps down to the bottom of the steps.

And I was still *so* hungry.

CHAPTER 27

The next morning Mom bounds into my room holding a newspaper. "Good morning, my rock star," she greets me. "Guess what?"

Rock star? She's tripping. I turn to look at her. My face says, *What?*

"You're famous!"

Huh?

She gets me out of bed, straps me into my chair, unplugs the Medi-Talker from the charger, and hooks me up. Then she places the morning paper on top of it.

There I sat plastered on the front page of the newspaper. In color.

"Wow!" I type.

"The article is all about the team winning the competition, but yours is the only picture they used. Interesting."

"Why me?"

Mom smiles quickly. "Because you are unique and wonderful and lots more interesting than ordinary fifth graders, I guess," she says. "The whole article seems to be focused on you."

"Team kids won't like that," I type.

"I'm sure they'll be happy for you, sweetheart."

"No, they won't."

"Here, listen to this."

She reads me the article: " 'Spaulding Street Elementary's talented academic team of fifth and sixth graders won the local Whiz Kids quiz competition last night by a score of eighty-six to eighty-five. With stunning skill and knowledge, they answered questions far above their grade level to defeat seven other teams.' "

"Makes us sound smart," I tap.

"And so you are," Mom replies.

"Math questions made me sweat." I get clammy under the arms just thinking about them.

Mom continues. "Ooh, here's the part about you. Listen to this! 'One outstanding member of the Spaulding team is Melody Brooks, an eleven-year-old who has been diagnosed with cerebral palsy. In spite of her physical challenges, Melody's quick and capable mental abilities were able to shine as she led her team to victory.' "

"They will hate me," I type glumly. Butterscotch, who still sleeps in my room, nuzzles my hand. She always seems to know how I feel, but it doesn't help this time.

"Oh, don't exaggerate. I think it's a lovely article, and your friends should be proud."

"You don't get it."

Mom ignores me and proceeds to get me ready for school. Two blue T-shirts — one to wear and one to pack, just in case. Two pairs of pants. She never picks out jeans. I decide not to argue. I have a feeling it is not going to be a good day.

"What a great photo of you! I'm going to make sure I get extra copies of the paper," she chatters cheerfully as she tugs on my socks before putting on my sneakers. "I've got to make sure everybody at work sees this."

Dad has finished dressing Penny, so he brings her into my room. When Penny notices my picture in the paper, she drops Doodle and shouts, "Dee-Dee!" She picks up the paper and kisses it.

I bet I won't get many reactions like that at school today.

Dad leans over and gives me a kiss on the cheek. "I'm so proud, I could pop," he says softly. "I love you, Melody."

That makes me get all teary. Just once I wish I could hug my little sister or tell my

258

dad I love him too. In real words, not through a machine.

The reaction at school today is just what I expected. Words float out of lips that say nice things to me, but eyes tell the truth. The eyes are cold, as if I had beat the reporter over the head and forced her to print that picture of me.

Even Rose acts distant. "Nice picture of you in the paper, Melody," she says.

"Thanks. Should have been all of us."

"I think so too," Rose replies.

I just sigh. *I can't do anything right. I don't want to be all that — I just want to be like everybody else.*

When we get to Mr. Dimming's class, he strides in wearing *another* brand-new suit — there must have been a two-for-one sale — and a brand-new smile. He looks like he might explode with happiness. He carries a stack of the morning newspaper with him.

"I didn't sleep at all last night," he admits to us. "I am just so *very* proud of our team and our school!"

He pauses while the class cheers for the quiz team. Rose, Molly, and Claire smile happily. Connor and Rodney take bows. A few kids even turn around and look at me with a smile.

"Do we get free pizza or something?"

Connor blurts out.

"Absolutely!" Mr. Dimming replies. "The principal has declared that next Friday is Quiz Team Day, and the entire school is being treated to free pizzas and sodas!"

More cheers from the class. Connor looks really pleased.

Mr. Dimming continues. "And I want to give a special shout-out to Melody, who really helped us secure our victory! Let's give her a special round of applause!"

He begins the clapping and the class joins in, but it seems more polite than sincere. I guess I'm not as cool as free pizza.

"Who saw the eleven o'clock news last night?" Mr. D asks, still beaming.

About half the kids raise their hands. I had missed it — I had fallen asleep exhausted after we got home.

"I taped it and TiVoed it and put it up on MySpace!" he tells us excitedly. "But now we must get back to regular class activities." He sounds disappointed.

"But how do we get ready for Washington?" Rose asks, obviously not ready to let him do that.

Teachers are *so* easily distracted! I knew he'd bite on that one.

Mr. Dimming smiles again and takes a deep breath. "We have only two weeks to get ready, Rose. I've prepared a packet for each of my team champs," he says as he passes out the paperwork. "Take this home and bring it back tomorrow without fail. In it I've included information about how to redeem the free plane tickets and info about our hotel and schedule for the days we are in D.C. It also gives details about our practice schedule, which begins today. We will meet every day after school and half a day on Saturday."

"Saturday?" Connor asks, disbelief in his voice.

I'm worried about that too. A whole half day? If Catherine can't come, how will I get to the bathroom or eat?

"I'll bring bagels for breakfast, fruit for snacks, and we'll order in burgers for lunch," Mr. Dimming tells him.

"Sounds sorta healthy," Connor responds with a grin. "But I'll be there."

"You skip a practice and you get bounced to the alternates, Connor. I'm in this to win."

"Why don't you take a couple of days off, my man?" Rodney says to Connor. "I'd be glad to take your place. Slide you right out in a blink." He sounds serious.

"No way, man. I'll show," Connor says hurriedly.

261

Molly raises her hand. "Mr. Dimming, do the alternates go to Washington also?"

"Absolutely!"

"So, should I buy a new dress just in case I get to be on the team?"

"That's up to you, Molly," the teacher replies.

Claire raises her hand then. "Mr. D, I think I know what Molly's getting at. Since there are six people on the D.C. team instead of four, which of the alternates will you choose?"

"We will use a point system," he replies. "The students with the six highest scores from all our preliminary rounds will make the final TV team. Sound fair?"

Claire looks satisfied at that, and she and Molly high-five each other.

Mr. Dimming finally gets back to regular class work — the study of Spain and Portugal — and I do my best to do nothing to call attention to myself. No weird noises or kicks or grunts for the rest of the class, no answers to questions I know. I just sit in the back of the room with Catherine and hope the morning will pass quickly.

I spend the afternoon in room H-5, where we watch Tom and Jerry cartoons for three hours. Can you *believe* it?

After school Catherine feeds me a pudding cup and some juice just before it's time to go to Mr. Dimming's room for our first practice. She frowns as I finish my last sip of juice.

"What's bugging you, Melody?" she asks. "You should be on top of the world, but you're acting like somebody just popped you in the nose."

"They don't want me on the team," I type.

"That's ridiculous. You were the star last night."

"That's the problem."

"Without you, they would not have won!"

"They're scared of me." I try to explain. **"They think I look funny."**

"You never let that bother you before," she counters.

It's hard to put my feelings into words that will come out right on my talker. I know the other kids are uncomfortable with me on the team. There's no other way to put it. My presence was cute at first, maybe okay for a local competition, but for the big game — on national television — that's different. I'll make them stand out, and not in a good way.

I start typing again. **"I make them look . . ."** I hesitate, then type in, **"weird."**

"You're the smartest person on the team!"

263

Catherine exclaims.

"I drool."

"So pack a box of tissues!"

"I make funny noises."

"And Connor farts sometimes!"

I have to smile at that.

"No more of this feeling sorry for yourself, young lady! Let's get down to Mr. D's room and kick some butt!"

"Okay, let's go," I type.

We roll down to the room, and I hold my head high. Well, at least as high as I can when it isn't wobbling around. Nobody says anything more about the newspaper article, and practice goes on as usual. I answer most of the questions correctly, and by the time Mom picks me up, I feel a little better.

But I do notice Rose and Claire and Molly whispering together as I leave. It could be about a new music video or a shopping trip to the mall . . . or it could be about me.

CHAPTER 28

How can they expect us to get ready in such a short time? Crazy! Plane tickets and permission slips. Paperwork and practice.

Practice every day for close to two weeks. Study every evening with Mrs. V. Words. Cities. States. Countries. Capitals. Oceans. Rivers. Colors. Diseases. Weather. Numbers. Dates. Animals. Kings. Queens. Birds. Insects. Wars. Presidents. Planets. Authors. Generals. Laws. Quotations. Measurements. Equations. Definitions. My head has been spinning nonstop with facts and figures. But I'm ready now. Our team is ready.

Mr. D kept his promise. The six highest scorers from all our practice rounds were announced at the last practice session a few days ago. Of course, just like the other kids, I had been keeping a mental tally of everybody's points, so I was pretty sure I'd be one of the on-air contestants, not an alternate.

Mr. Dimming almost *glowed* with antici-pation as he made the announcement. He paced nervously. A little more and the man would be dancing!

"Here we go," he said. "I feel like I need a drumroll or something!"

"Read the list — please!" Connor shouted impatiently.

Mr. Dimming said slowly, "The six mem-bers of the championship Spaulding Street Elementary School quiz team are . . ." He paused. I thought Connor was going to throw something at him. "Rose, Connor, Melody, Elena, Rodney, and Molly. Claire and Amanda will be our alternates."

"I'm an alternate?" Claire gasped.

"Molly beat you by two points, Claire," Mr. D explained. "But you still get to come with us and cheer us on and tour the city."

"But it was *me* who helped her study!" Claire said, outrage in her voice. "That is so *not* fair!"

I just shook my head and smiled a little. There is *so* much Claire doesn't know about stuff not being fair.

Molly looked smug and not at all sorry. Her mother came to pick her up, and the practice was over.

The competition is tomorrow — Thursday evening. Assuming we win, we'll have the

266

Good Morning America appearance on Friday, followed by a trip to the White House. More sightseeing in D.C. is planned for Saturday, then we come home on Sunday. On Monday, hopefully, we'll return to school as national champions. With that trophy.

So tonight we pack. I've never been on a trip away from home before, so we have some serious planning to do. I feel crazy excited, crazy nervous. Dad bought me a bright red suitcase with wheels. It smells like the inside of a new car. Touching it makes me smile.

Mom and I went shopping yesterday — something we don't get to do much anymore. She let me choose a couple of new outfits — with *jeans* — none of those practical, baggy sweat suits for this trip!

As we rolled down the mall, we passed a card shop. I had a brainstorm and tapped out on my board, **"Go in. Get card, please."**

"For whom?" Mom asked as we wheeled in there.

"Catherine," I typed. **"To thank her. For helping me get ready."**

"How very grown up of you!" Mom said, clearly pleased.

"One for Mrs. V, too?" I tapped out.

"Absolutely!"

The card we found for Mrs. V could not have been more perfect. The front was completely covered with hundreds of oranges, except for one blue one in the middle. Inside, it said: *You're one in a million. Thanks.*

"She'll love it," Mom said.

For Catherine, I picked out a card that showed a desk full of computers and MP3 players and video games, and a young woman connected to all of them with earphones. It read: *Glad you're always there to plug in to me. Thanks for all you do.*

"You couldn't have designed those better yourself," Mom said as she paid for the cards. Yep, pretty perfect.

Around seven o'clock the doorbell rings. It's Mrs. V, coming over to help with the final packing preparations. She and Mom make a great team.

"I've made a checklist according to Mr. Dimming's suggestions," Mom says. "Black skirt and white blouse for the competition."

"Check," Mrs. V says as she neatly folds those two pieces into my suitcase.

"Sheck!" Penny mimics.

"Extra white blouse, just in case," Mom says.

"Great idea," Mrs. V replies, nodding.

Mom carefully folds in two more shirts and my favorite pair of jeans. "Comfortable outfits for sightseeing in Washington. Spending money for souvenirs. Sunglasses. Camera."

"Check, check, check," Mrs. V repeats.

"Pajamas, toothbrush, deodorant, hair clips."

"All there."

"A warm jacket — no telling what this March weather will do."

"Sheck!" Penny cries.

"Power pack for Medi-Talker, extra batteries, tissues, and wipes."

"Got it!"

"Umbrella?"

"For you or for Melody?" Mrs. V asks with a laugh. "Do you have *your* bag packed?"

"Yeah, I'm just about ready. I'm nervous too." Mom pauses. "You're the best, Violet. I know Penny will be safe with you while we're gone —"

"And Butterscotch," I interrupt.

They both laugh. Mom continues, "Frankly, without you, there is no way that Melody would be packing for this trip."

"Get card, Mom," I type. I reach my hand to the side, but I can barely touch the edge of my book bag hanging on my chair.

Mom reaches into the bag, pulls out the

envelope, and sets it on my tray. I push it toward Mrs. V.

She opens it, reads it, then squeezes me so hard, I can hardly catch my breath. "This one goes on my refrigerator door!" she says quietly. "I want to look at it every single day." She busies herself then with dusting off a pair of my shoes that have never taken a step.

"I'm a little scared," I admit.

"Nonsense, Mello Yello," Mrs. V tells me. "I fully expect to see you on *Good Morning America* with that ten-foot-high trophy!"

"That would be awesome," I type.

"Now tell me once more," Mrs. V says to Mom. "What time does the plane leave tomorrow? Penny, take Melody's underwear off your head, you silly girl!"

Mom checks her papers. "Plane leaves at noon. That means we should leave here no later than nine, get to the airport by ten, get all checked in, make sure her wheelchair is properly taken care of and such, then we can relax until it's time to board the plane."

Mrs. V scratches her head. "I wonder why they chose the noon flight. That will get you into Washington around two. The competition starts at seven. That's cutting it a little close."

"Mr. Dimming told us the hotel has a late

check-in policy. The TV studio is just across the street from the hotel, so we'll be fine."

As Mom closes and zips my suitcase, I feel tears come into my eyes. I can't believe this is happening. In just one day I will be in Washington, D.C., on national television. I pray I won't screw up.

I want to call Rose and see if she's nervous too. I want to ask her what she'll wear to the White House. Suppose we get to meet the First Lady — now, that would be the bomb! I want to know if we'll be sitting near each other on the plane. I want to be like all the other girls.

I don't sleep well that night. In the morning Mom gets me bathed and dressed and fed in record time while Dad gets Penny ready.

"Go see plane?" she asks repeatedly.

"Fly! Whee!" Dad says as he flies her around the room in his arms. She loves it.

We head outside, and Mrs. V hurries over, camera in hand. She snaps pictures of me getting strapped in, my suitcase being loaded, and my brave and hopeful victory smile. Then she does it all over again with Dad's camcorder. No, we'll never be able to forget this morning.

Penny darts about, chasing Butterscotch, running in circles around the car, which has been washed and shined. Mom, dressed in a cool denim suit and, surprisingly, a pair of late-style Nikes, loads our bags in the car, and we're totally ready to go by eight forty-five.

Dad takes Butterscotch back into the house, then locks the front door on his way out. "All set?" he asks.

"Let's do it!" Mom yells. Even Penny can feel the excitement. She claps her hands. I can't stop grinning.

Even though I know we have plenty of time, I keep wanting Dad to drive faster. I'm so afraid that we'll miss the plane or that we forgot my ticket or that I'll throw up and we'll have to go back home.

At the airport garage we have no trouble finding a row of empty handicapped parking spaces. We unload me, my chair, our bags, and Penny and Doodle. Mrs. V snaps more photos.

It seems like hours, but in minutes we're at the check-in gate.

Mrs. V pushes me. Mom carries Penny. Dad pulls a cart loaded with the luggage and Doodle. It's ten o'clock on the dot.

"Hi!" Mom says cheerfully to the uni-formed lady at the desk. "We're here to check in for the noon flight to Washington, D.C." She hands the lady our tickets.

"The noon flight?" the woman replies with a frown. She types and clicks, purses her lips, then types some more. Finally, she looks up. "I'm sorry, ma'am, but that flight has been cancelled. We've had loads of cancellations today — a late-winter snowstorm in the Northeast has caused backups all over."

Cancelled? My stomach starts to gurgle.

"Snow?" Mom's voice sounds thick. "But the weather here is sunny and clear."

"They've got five inches on the ground in Boston already, and more is predicted for this afternoon farther south. The FAA won't let planes take off in weather like that, so our whole system gets gummed up. Planes due to arrive here and then return eastward get cancelled, meaning our afternoon flights can't depart. It's complicated. Sorry."

The desk agent continues to type rapidly. She tells Mom, "I can get you and your daughter on the next direct flight out, however. It leaves here at 7:23 p.m. and will get you into Washington at 9:07. The weather service has predicted that the storm system will have fizzled by then, so we can start getting folks where they need to be. Actually, tomorrow it will all be rain."

My heart is thudding now.

"Would you like me to rebook you now?"

273

She smiles cheerfully. She doesn't get it.

"But the competition *starts* at seven," Mom mumbles weakly.

"Excuse me? I didn't hear you," the desk agent says.

I can't breathe.

Mom speaks a little louder. "What about the rest of our group? We're traveling together — a group of schoolchildren — a quiz team, actually. They were also booked on this flight. We've got a competition this evening."

"Oh, I remember those kids. They were here early this morning. Great group. So polite and well mannered. They told me all about the competition and the huge trophy they might be bringing home."

"They came *early*?" Mom croaks.

"It seems they all went to breakfast together, then came straight here. It's a good thing they did too, or they wouldn't have gotten out."

"Where are they?" Mom asks.

"Oh, they got switched to the nine o'clock flight — the last eastbound plane to get out before flights started getting cancelled. They had to run down to the gate, but they made it just in time. I made sure of it." She looks down at her computer. "Yes, that flight left about an hour ago."

"They're gone?" Mom whispers.

I feel like I'm going to choke.

"Are you and your family going to D.C. to cheer them on?" the woman asks. She still doesn't get it.

"No, my daughter is on the team," Mom explains. "We *must* get to Washington. Isn't there another flight — perhaps on another airline?"

The woman looks at me and blinks. "She's on the . . . ?" she starts to ask, but then she catches herself, returns her gaze to her monitor, and begins typing furiously once more. I can hear her fingernails as they click on the keys.

Dad places both hands on the ticket counter and leans in toward the agent. I've never seen him so angry. "How could this happen? Shouldn't we have been notified that the flight was cancelled?"

"We try, sir, but it's not always possible," the lady replies, sounding truly sorry. "We do always advise passengers to call ahead and check their flight status."

"But this was the trip of a lifetime! You can't possibly understand how important this is to my daughter!"

I squeeze my eyes shut. Stupid elevator music floats from the tinny airport speakers. I hear no beautiful colors. I smell no lovely aromas. All I can see is the darkness behind my eyeballs.

"I'm really, really sorry, sir," the lady says.

"What about a connecting flight? We *must* get her to Washington this afternoon!"

The woman types and clicks for what seems like hours. Finally, she looks up. "There are no other flights to D.C. on any other carrier, sir, nonstop or otherwise. That weather system has grounded everything. There will be nothing until later this evening. I'm so sorry," she whispers.

I open my eyes because they are filling with tears.

Dad walks away from the ticket counter, his face scrunched into tight wrinkles, then, without warning, he smashes his fist into the wall right next to where I'm sitting.

I jerk my head up. I know that had to hurt.

"Ahhh! I shouldn't have done that!" he admits, holding one fist in the other.

But if I could have smashed my fist against a wall, I would have as well.

Mrs. V looks from Dad to me. "I don't understand how this could have happened either," she says to Mom. "Shouldn't someone from the quiz team have called you?" Her voice could crush bricks. "The teacher, perhaps?"

"Maybe there wasn't time," Mom says

helplessly. "At least that's what I hope. Surely they . . . surely they wouldn't have left her behind on purpose."

I still have not taken one deep breath.

"I really do apologize, ma'am," the gate agent finally says. "I've even checked airports in nearby cities. There are no flights out of the area until this evening. I have plenty of seats on our seven o'clock flight if you'd like me to book you."

"No, thank you," Mom says quietly. "It's too late."

The entire airport feels like a vacuum to me. No sound. No voices. No air.

Mom walks slowly toward me.

I sit there in my new blue and white outfit with new matching tennis shoes, next to my new shiny red suitcase, feeling very, very stupid.

And angry. How could they *do* this to me?

And helpless. I *hate* feeling like this — like when I was little and got stuck on my back like a stupid turtle. There was nothing I could do. Nothing.

"How long does it take to drive to D.C.?" Mrs. V asks. I don't even look up. I know the answer.

"Ten hours at the very least," Dad replies, his voice soft.

"Go fly airplane?" Penny asks.

"No fly today," Dad says, touching her gently on her head with his good hand.

Mom rolls me over to a bench on the other side of the check-in area. She kneels down in front of me. She's crying.

I don't think I'll ever breathe again.

Mom hugs me. "It's gonna be okay, sweetie. You're still the best, the smartest, the most wonderful girl in the world. Somehow we're going to get over this."

No. I won't.

Mrs. V wipes her eyes as well. She sits on the bench and takes both my hands in hers. "Oh, baby girl, I know this is hard. But there is just no way to get you to Washington."

I just sit there. The morning started out like crystal, but the day has turned to broken glass.

CHAPTER 29

When we get home, I ask my mother to put me in bed. I refuse to eat lunch. I try to sleep, but quiz questions and why questions keep flying into my head.

Why didn't they call me?

Why didn't they tell me about breakfast?

Why can't I be like everybody else?

I finally cry into my pillow. Butterscotch nudges me with her nose, but I ignore her.

They left me on purpose! How could they do that? They left me on purpose!

I feel like stomping on something. Stomping and stomping and *stomping!* That makes me even crazier because I can't even do that! I can't even get *mad* like a normal kid.

Penny peeks into my room, then, when she sees I'm awake, she climbs up on my bed and snuggles close to me. She smells like watermelon bubble bath. She tries to count my fingers, then tries to count her own, but all she knows is one, two, three, five, so she says that over and over. Then she tries to teach Doodle to count. "Two, Doodle! Two!" I feel myself relaxing a tiny bit.

"Oh, here you are, Penny!" Dad says from my doorway. "Are you making Dee-Dee happy?"

"Dee-Dee good girl," she tells Dad.

"Yes, she is that. The very best," Dad agrees. "You okay, Melody?" he asks as he comes over to stroke my hair.

I nod. I point to Dad's left wrist, which is wrapped in an Ace bandage.

"Yeah, it hurts," he says. "That was a dumb thing to do, but I guess it made me feel better."

I nod again.

He lifts Penny from my bed with his right arm. "Ready for a snack, Miss Penny?" he asks her.

"Hot dogs!" she demands.

"Do you want me to fix you something, Melody?" he asks me.

I'm not hungry. I shake my head, then point to the clock.

"Maybe later?" Dad says.

I smile at him, and he quietly leaves the room with my sister.

The phone rings.

I hear Mom say, "Oh, hello, Mr. Dimming." She walks quickly into my room, portable phone to her ear, her palm so tight around the receiver, I can see the veins on the top of her hand.

"No, I *don't* understand," Mom says curtly. "Why weren't we called?" She listens to him for a minute, then bursts out angrily, "We could have easily been at the airport an hour earlier. We could have been there at dawn!" She's almost shouting. "Do you know how much this has devastated my daughter?"

A pause.

"Yes, I'm aware she's probably the brightest person on the team. Was. The word is WAS. There is no IS." Mom pauses to listen again. "*You'll make it up to her?* You've got to be kidding!"

Mom hangs up on him and flings the phone into a corner. She wipes her eyes, pulls a tissue from a box on my desk, and sits down heavily on the chair next to my bed. I listen to her blow her nose, then I turn over.

"Oh, Melody, if only I could make your hurt go away," she says plaintively.

I blink at my own tears.

She pulls me up onto her lap. It isn't the snuggly fit it used to be, but it feels good. She rocks me, humming softly. I finally fall

asleep listening to the rhythm of her heartbeat.

CHAPTER 30

What happened today was all my fault. I should have listened. We should have all stayed home and spent the day together. But we didn't. Because of me.

When I awoke this morning, it was raining. Thunder. Lightning. Wind. A constant, soaking downpour that laughed at umbrellas and raincoats. The air itself was gray and heavy, thick with too much moisture. I could hear it pounding on my window.

Dad came into my room and sat down in our old reading chair. He held his wrist carefully. Mom had put his arm in a sling. "Messy day out there," he said.

I nodded.

"Your team got beat in one of the late rounds in D.C. last night," he told me. "They got ninth place — a little bitty trophy."

But they weren't *my* team anymore. I tried to pretend like I didn't care. I blinked real hard and faced the wall.

"I wish I could fix this for you, Melody," Dad said quietly as he headed out of my room.

That made the tears fall for real.

At first I didn't want to go to school. I'd been excused because I was supposed to be in Washington, and if I went in, I'd have to sit all day in room H-5 with Willy and Maria and Freddy. It seemed pointless.

But as I thought about it, I changed my mind. I felt the sorry for myself shift to mad again. And the mad me decided that I was *not* going to sit at home like a kicked-around puppy. I was gonna show up and let everybody know they didn't beat me.

Mom leaned on my door just then and said, "You want to stay home today? No one will blame you."

I shook my head forcefully. *No! No! No!* I kicked the covers off my feet.

She sighed. "Okay, okay. But the weather is ugly, and I woke up with a migraine. Plus, Penny is sick, and Butterscotch threw up on the carpet. I had to put her in the basement."

She got me bathed and dressed and took me downstairs. Usually, Dad carries me up and down the steps, but with his arm out of commission, Mom just grunted, lifted me, and did it herself. She eased me into my manual chair (my electric chair and lightning storms don't mix well), hooked up my old Plexiglas talking board (ditto for Elvira), then sat down to catch her breath.

"It looks like we're going to have one stormy day, honey," she said as she glanced at the wet mess outside the window. As she ran a brush through my hair, she whispered, "I'm so sorry, my Melody, so, so sorry about everything."

I reached up and touched her hand.

The rain continued to fall.

She fixed me breakfast — scrambled eggs and Cream of Wheat — and fed me, one spoonful at a time. She kept placing her palm against her forehead. She was unusually quiet. I wondered if she was thinking about how many times she had fed me, how many more times she'd have to do it.

Wearing a floppy yellow hat and yellow duck-footed sleepers, Penny wandered into the kitchen, coughing and sneezing.

Mom stopped feeding me, found a Kleenex, and wiped Penny's nose. She hated that, of course, so she screamed like she was being tortured by enemy spies. Normally, Mom makes a game of it and wipes Doodle's nose as well to make Penny tolerate it better, but I guess she didn't feel up to it this time.

Then the phone rang. Mom answered, a spoon in one hand, the dirty Kleenex in the other.

"Hello. You what? You need me to come in? But I'm off today. I'm supposed to be in Washington." She paused. "Long story."

I cringed. Penny continued to howl.

She ought to put Penny in the basement with the dog! I thought, frowning.

Butterscotch scratched furiously at the basement door.

"Penny, please!" Mom cried out, cupping her hand over the phone. "I can't hear!"

Penny quieted a little, but only because she had squatted down on the floor and put both hands in Butterscotch's water bowl — sloshing water all over the floor.

Mom listened for a minute, then said into the phone, "How bad is the accident? Lots of injuries? Okay, I understand. I'll be there, but I have to wait until I get my daughter on the school bus."

She hung up the phone and sighed, squeezing the tissue into her fist.

"I've got to go in to the hospital, Chuck," she called out to Dad. "Big pileup on the freeway. Are you dressed and ready?"

Dad came downstairs, still in his pajamas. "I'm not going in today," he announced.

286

"You almost never take a day off," Mom said, a surprised frown on her face.

"My wrist is aching, the weather is awful, and Penny has a cold," he explained. "Why don't you just stay home with me today?" he said to me.

But no, I kicked and shrieked and insisted on going to school. **Can't miss today!** I pointed. **Must go! Must go!**

Mom just put her head in her hands once more. "Get Penny out of the dog's dish" was all she finally said.

Dad ripped a bunch of paper towels from the roll, cleaned up Penny's mess, and wiped her nose with a wet paper towel. That started her screaming again. Her screech became a shriek.

That's when she reached up and knocked over the cup of orange juice on my tray. My clean blouse was a soppy mess. *She did that on purpose!* I thought angrily.

Mom simply shrugged her shoulders and yanked off my shirt in one swift motion. She told Dad, "Melody is determined to show up at school — why, I do not know — but she may as well go."

I couldn't explain to them that I wanted to see Catherine. Somehow I felt like she'd talk to me and make me feel better. She's a college kid — she would know what to say.

287

Besides, I had to give her that card. Today.

It took Mom several minutes to find a new shirt for me until she remembered all the clean clothes in my suitcase. When she rolled that red suitcase into the kitchen, I looked at her, then looked away. I refused to cry any more.

For some reason, the bus came early that morning. I'd just gotten my clean shirt on, my book bag still needed to be packed with my lunch and Catherine's card, and I had to go to the bathroom. Even over the noise of all the rain and thunder, the honk of the bus horn blared clearly. It always sounds like a goose in pain.

I heard Dad open the front door to wave the driver on. He yelled, "Don't wait, Gus! She's not ready!" The driver — a sandy-haired guy who's been on this route for a couple of years — beeped once more, then rumbled on. Gus is really cool and often waits a few minutes as parents hustle to get their children out of their houses. It just takes us longer sometimes to get it together in the morning.

"Melody, baby, why don't you just stay home with Dad and Penny today? Please?" Mom asked as she lifted me off the toilet. "It's such an icky day."

I kicked and cried out again, shaking my

head. *No, no, no!* I didn't know why it was so important, but I knew I had to show up. Maybe I wanted to let everybody know what the team had done to me — I wasn't really sure. I only knew I had to go to school.

Mom sighed and pulled up my jeans. When I got back in my chair, I pointed to **Thanks** and **Mom**. She just shook her head and stuffed my lunch into my book bag.

The rain didn't seem to be letting up, so Mom took a deep breath and started the process of loading me into the car. When I ride the bus, I simply roll down our ramp, down the driveway, onto the bus lift, and into a specially designed area of the bus that straps my chair into place.

But when I ride in the car, it involves a whole process of taking apart and putting together me, my chair, and my stuff. Even with my manual chair, it's a pain.

And Dad was no help. With his arm in a sling, he shrugged and tried to look like he was sorry he couldn't come out and lend Mom a hand. I think he was enjoying it a little, and that made Mom even more upset.

The rain and wind, if anything, had gotten worse. Mom had draped a huge plastic raincoat over me and my chair, and another one over herself, but in seconds the hoods had blown off and our heads were soaked.

We headed slowly down the wheelchair ramp, the wind whipping at us and the rain attacking from all sides.

I thought it was exciting. I'd never seen the sky so dark at eight in the morning. The thunder and wind made it feel like a scene out of a really good movie. My hair is short and curly, and I think it looks sorta cute when it's wet. Good thing. Mom hates it when her hair gets wet — it gets stringy and limp. I gotta admit: Mom with wet hair should hide in a closet.

She opened the car door on the passenger side, and the wind blew it shut. She did it again, this time using me and my chair as a doorstop. The front seat of the car, of course, was getting soaked. She lifted me into the seat, strapped me in, and began the process of collapsing my chair. Fortunately, most of it is plastic and leather and metal, but I knew it would stay damp all day, even if somebody wiped it off real good when I got to school.

Mom placed my chair, along with my old communication board, into the back of the SUV. When she shut the trunk, she slammed it hard. The rain continued to fall. By the time she scooted into the driver's seat, she was a dripping mess and in a terrible mood.

"I wish I could go back to bed," she said

grumpily as she put the key into the ignition. "My head is killing me — why did I agree to go to work? I'm supposed to be off today, with you in Washington." She sighed heavily.

I kicked my legs in response, but only a little. I didn't want to upset her even more. That's when I glanced down and noticed she'd forgotten my book bag. *Catherine's card!* I reached over, grabbed Mom's arm, and pointed to my feet.

"What?" she said, irritation in her voice.

I kicked, I pointed, I grunted. Then I pointed to the house. Dad, who had changed into thick gray sweats, was standing there at the front door, grinning, my denim book bag in his right hand. I could see Penny, still in her little yellow duck pajamas and now a yellow rain hat, standing behind him. She had Doodle and Mom's red umbrella in her hands. Lightning crackled. Thunder followed. The rain poured. I watched Mom's hands tighten on the steering wheel.

She made a noise that sounded like something I would say, almost a growl. *"Arrrrh!"* She flung open the car door, stomped back out into the storm, up the ramp, and then she snatched the book bag from Dad. She was sopping by the time she got back in the car. Dad waved his bandaged arm from the porch one last time, then turned and went back into the dryness of the house. I watched as the front door *almost* closed.

That's when I saw a small bundle of yellow, dragging a red umbrella, dart out of the house. I saw her for only a second. But I saw.

I screamed! I kicked! I flailed my arms!

The windows were almost completely fogged up, and they got even worse as I continued to act like I'd been possessed by demons. Mom looked at me as if I had lost my mind. She screamed at me, "Stop it! Are you crazy?"

But I wouldn't stop. I couldn't. I banged on the car window, pulled Mom's shirt, hit her head. I pinched her, or at least tried to.

"I can't take any more, Melody!" Mom screamed over the thunder. "I *hate* it when you get like this. You've got to learn to control yourself! Now QUIT!" She put her hand on the keys to start the car.

I screamed, reached over, and tried to pull the keys from her. I scratched the back of Mom's hand.

She smacked me on the leg. She'd never raised a hand to me before. Never. I still didn't stop screaming and kicking and jerking. I had to tell her. *I had to tell her that*

Penny was out there! Never had I wanted words more.

I was going out of my mind.

"I'm taking you to school, and I hope they keep you!" Mom mumbled under her breath. Angrily, she turned on the car. A rush of air started to clear the windows. The windshield wipers rocked at their fastest speed.

I cried. Huge, sobbing tears. I grabbed at Mom's arms once more, but all she did was shake my arm away. I could tell she felt like hitting me again, but she didn't. Her lips were tight. She looked out the rearview mirror. She put the car into reverse.

I shrieked, I screeched, I yelled. The rain poured. The thunder roared.

Slowly, the big car rolled backward. I felt the soft thud. I became deadly silent.

Mom stopped, turning her head slowly to the left. Then she turned slowly to the right, almost as if in slow motion, as she saw Dad come running out of the house, a look of stark alarm on his face. "Penny!" I heard him yell. "Where's Penny?"

Mom rolled the window down on my side. Rain poured in onto me, but I didn't care. "What do you mean? She's with you!" Mom's voice was low, but sounded frantic and very, very scared.

She got out of the car. She looked down. She screamed for a long, long time.

Her screams were louder than the police sirens that eventually came shrieking around our corner, louder than the fire truck and ambulance sirens that followed them, louder than my silent cries.

I sat there for what seemed like hours, basically forgotten, strapped in the front seat of the car as the rain poured in my open window.

I ached with fear.

CHAPTER 31

The air felt thick and damp, like the silence that followed the screaming and crying and sirens. The rain had slowed to a drizzle.

After Mom and Dad left with the ambulance, Mrs. V took me out of the car and sat me in my chair. She placed the soggy, filthy Doodle on my tray.

"I found this under the car," she said, her voice shaky.

I touched it and burst into tears.

As she rolled me to her house, she said, "We're gonna clean Doodle up and have him waiting for Penny when she comes home. You hear?" I couldn't tell if she was trying to convince me or herself.

I felt dizzy and nauseous. I could not stop shaking.

After changing my clothes into warm, dry sweats, she switched the radio to an easy-listening station and turned the volume down low. The only color I heard was gray.

Mrs. V stood behind me, gently rubbing my shoulders.

"Are you hungry?" she asked.

I shook my head no.

She continued to massage my back and shoulders until we both could feel the tension slipping away.

"I'm going next door to get your Medi-Talker and the dog," she said. "You want anything else?"

I shook my head and continued to listen to the tones of smoky gray.

When she got back, Butterscotch seemed nervous. She kept pacing and sniffing, as if she was looking for something.

"I think she's looking for Penny," Mrs. V said. "Dogs know."

She hooked up Elvira to my chair and switched it on, but there was nothing either of us could say.

"It's not your fault, you know," she said finally.

I shook my head forcefully. Mrs. V should know better than to say stuff just to make me feel better.

"I mean it, Melody. It is *not* your fault!"

"Yes, it is!" I replied on my talker. I turned the volume up loud.

Mrs. V walked around to where I could see her, leaned down until her face was just inches from my own. "You did your best to warn your mother. You should be proud of yourself."

"Not proud. Not enough," I typed.

"Sometimes things happen that are beyond our control, Melody. You did everything right."

The guilt bubbled up then.

"I was mad at Penny," I typed, slower than usual.

"Penny knows you love her," she said.

Tears slid down my cheeks.

"Made Mom take me to school."

"So what? The fact that you insisted on going to school, even after what happened to you yesterday, shows you are a strong person, a better person than anyone else there. I'm proud of you for that."

"Don't be."

"I'm sure Penny will be just fine," Mrs. V said then, but her voice said otherwise. For the first time I could remember, Mrs. V sounded unsure.

"Will she die?" I had to know.

"She was alive and breathing when the ambulance took her, so I'm going to believe that's still the case. Toddlers are very resilient, you know."

I had to know something else. **"Her brain? Messed up?"** I asked. I had seen enough television shows on brain trauma to know it was possible. My classmate Jill had been in a car accident. I couldn't bear to see Penny like that.

Mrs. V answered thoughtfully and honestly. "I suppose it's possible, but I pray that's not the case."

"Two broken kids," I typed. Just the idea almost made me gag.

"That's not gonna happen, Melody." But Mrs. V's voice wavered — I heard it.

I was still for a moment, then I typed, **"It should have been me."**

"Huh? What do you mean?"

"Nobody would miss me."

"Now, you just stop stupid talk like that! My whole world would fall apart if something happened to you. Your parents' as well."

I'm not sure I believed her. I tilted my head. **"Really?"** I typed.

"I plan to wear purple to your college graduation!"

"Far away and very hard."

"Like making the quiz team?"

"They left me."

"And they lost!"

I glanced out of her large picture window and watched the wet branches sway. How could I say it? I looked back at my talker and typed very slowly, **"I want to be like other kids."**

"So you want to be mean and fake and thoughtless?"

I looked up at her angry face, then looked away. **"No. Normal."**

"Normal sucks!" she roared. "People love you because you're Melody, not because of what you can or cannot do. Give us a little credit."

"I want it to be yesterday," I typed.

"Yesterday your heart was broken because they left you behind, remember?"

"Rather have that than this."

"I know. Oh, Melody, I know."

"I'm scared."

"Me too."

The silent room echoed our thoughts.

"I had a goldfish. He jumped out of his bowl," I typed then.

"I remember your mom telling me about that."

"Tried to save him. Couldn't."

The phone rang then, startling both of us. I jerked in my chair. Mrs. V picked it up.

"Yes," she said.

I strained to listen.

"Oh, no!" she said.

My heart dropped beneath my chair. She listened for a long time.

"Oh, yes!" she said finally. Then she burst into tears and hung up.

"Is Penny dead?" I typed. The world was spinning.

Mrs. V wiped her eyes, looked at me, and took a deep breath. "She has some internal injuries, a badly broken leg, but she survived the surgery! She's gonna live!" Then she cried once more.

Normal doesn't suck at all.

CHAPTER 32

It's Monday, so I have to return to school today. The temperature has dropped and the sun is glowing like some kind of frosted golden jewel. Yet everything feels different and not quite right.

Mom spent the weekend at the hospital with Penny, sleeping on a cot in her room. I have not seen her since, well, since everything changed. I wonder if Mom is mad at me.

Mrs. V comes over and helps me get dressed and fed. Even Butterscotch seems to miss Penny. She puts her head in my lap and looks at me with lonely eyes. I can't help her.

Dad is a mess. He keeps dropping things like forks and keys. He starts to talk, then forgets what he was going to say. He hasn't shaved.

"Go and get yourself together, Chuck," Mrs. V finally tells him. "A hot shower and cold glass of orange juice will do you wonders. When you go see Penny this morning, you don't want to scare the child, do you?"

"Uh, you're right," Dad replies. "You've got Melody covered?"

"I'll see she gets on the bus. Now scoot!"

He bounds up the stairs to the bathroom.

"Penny better?" I tap on my board.

"Yes, oh, yes! When I spoke to your mom this morning, she told me that they have taken her off the IV already. Penny was eating applesauce, complaining about her cast, and asking for Doodle, which I've got cleaned up and ready for her. Penny is going to be fine, Melody. Just fine."

I inhale deeply. Mrs. V spoons eggs into my mouth, but my stomach roils with worry.

"Her leg?" I ask.

"Her leg is in a cast. It's big and clunky and will annoy the heck out of her, but the doctors have said that when she gets stronger, she'll even be able to walk with it."

I'm glad Mrs. V is always straight up with me.

"Wheelchair?" I can't think of anything worse than a teeny baby wheelchair.

"No. They want her to move around as much as possible."

I breathe a sigh of relief. **"Her head?"** I ask.

Mrs. V understands. "No brain damage, Melody. None."

I exhale slowly. **"You sure?"** I spell out.

"Absolutely. I saw her myself last night. She bumped her head when she fell, but the car hit her leg. It didn't touch her head at all."

The school bus honks then, so Mrs. V wheels me down the drive to meet it.

She checks my backpack, adjusts my foot straps, and gives me a big hug.

"You ready, Melody? Ready to face the quiz team?"

I nod. After what had almost happened, facing a bunch of snotty fifth graders will be easy.

Gus looks at me with concern as he lowers the bus lift.

"How's your little sister?" he asks me. "That is so scary!"

"Gonna be okay," I type. **"Thanks."**

I realize right then that news like that travels fast. Everybody at school will probably know as well.

Gus wheels me onto the lift and pushes the button to raise it as I wave good-bye to Mrs. V. The ride to school is strangely quiet — none of the usual squeaks and grunts from the students who ride the special bus.

When we get to school, the air is chilly, so the aides take us directly to room H-5. As we get settled, I look at my friends there through different eyes.

Freddy, who wants to zoom to the moon.

Ashley, our fashion model.

Willy, the baseball expert.

Maria, who has no enemies.

Gloria, the music lover.

Carl, our resident gourmet.

Jill, who might have once been like Penny.

Not one of them even knows how to be mean.

And me, the dreamer who tries to escape room H-5, a kid with a computer named Elvira. I don't even know where I belong anymore.

Catherine comes in then, wearing a new outfit that is actually cute and stylish. Tan slacks, black sweater, and a vest.

"Nice outfit," I tell her.

"Thanks! And I did it all by myself."

"I have something for you." I point to my book bag.

She reaches into my bag, digs around, and finds the card that almost led to tragedy. After she reads it, she blinks back tears.

"No, Melody, thank *you*!" She leans over and hugs me. Then she looks serious and says, "Mrs. Valencia called and told me all about what happened with your little sister. How's she doing?"

"Better," I type.

"You know, you probably saved her life," Catherine tells me.

"What?"

"Seriously. Your screaming and yelling slowed your mother down. Gave her time to figure out why you were acting like you had hot potatoes in your pants."

"Could not stop Mom," I stab out on my machine.

"You did exactly the right thing. I'm so proud of you."

"Really?"

"Really. Especially after all you had been through at the airport. You want to talk about it?"

"No," I type, and look away.

Maria comes over to my chair and gives me a big hug. "You did good, Melly-Belly," she says. "Real good."

I'm not sure if she is talking about the quiz team or something else, but my eyes get all drippy and my nose starts to run.

I wish I could give her a big squeeze back to let her know how good she has made me feel. But I just tap, **"Thanks."**

I'm never sure how much Freddy is aware

of what's going on in the world around him, so he surprises me when he zips over to me and asks, "Melly go zoom in plane?" He looks excited, maybe even envious.

"No, Freddy," I type. **"No plane. No zoom."**

His face scrunches up into sadness, then he drives away.

Mrs. Shannon comes over next and squats beside me. "Your head must be near 'bout ready to explode from all that's happened in the past few days."

"Boom," I type. But I don't feel like smiling.

"Let's talk at lunch. Okay, Melody?"

"Okay."

"Are you going to your inclusion classes?" she asks.

"Yes," I tap. I'd thought about this all weekend — when I wasn't thinking about Penny. I'd decided I wasn't going to hide.

"I want you to know I'm very proud of you." She gives me a big thumbs-up and then gets our morning routine going.

As it turns out, Miss Gordon is absent today, so the first inclusion class I'm set to attend is Mr. Dimming's.

"Are you sure you want to go?" Catherine asks me. Instead of answering, I power my chair toward Mr. D's door. Catherine rests

306

a hand on my shoulder as I whir in.

A small brass-colored trophy sits on Mr. D's desk. The room is quieter than normal.

Mr. Dimming clears his throat. He shifts from one foot to the other. He runs his finger around the collar of his dim white shirt — he's back to his old, well-worn brown suit. His old shoes as well.

Finally, he says, "Hello, Melody!" His voice sounds fake cheerful.

I do not reply.

He wiggles so much, he looks like he has to go to the bathroom. I just watch him. No kicks from me. No weird sounds. I am amazingly calm.

I glance over at Rose, but she is looking in the other direction. No one seems to know what to say.

At last I break the silence. I turn the volume up loud on my machine, then type out, **"Why did you leave me?"**

Somebody should have been there with a video camera proving that, yes, a fifth-grade classroom can be absolutely, totally quiet.

Faces search other faces, each one willing another to speak.

Eventually, Rose stands up. She looks directly at me and says, "We didn't plan to leave you, Melody. Honest."

I look her dead in the eye and wait.

307

I don't react at all. I just wait.

She continues. "We all went out to breakfast early that morning —"

I interrupt. **"Nobody told me about that. How come?"**

None of them answer. Their silence says what their words cannot — it's better without me.

I blink real fast.

Claire finally stammers, "We figured you'd slow us down because you have to be fed and stuff."

It's so quiet, I swear I can hear my own heartbeat.

"You threw up. Nobody left you."

"Ooh, snap!" I hear Rodney whisper.

Claire stares down at her desk.

"Who took my place?"

Claire lifts her hand slightly, but she won't look at me.

Rose scrapes at a spot on her history book. "We finished breakfast really fast because we were all excited, so we got to the airport extra early."

Connor stands up then. He looks uncomfortable. "So when we got to the airport, they told us that the noon flight had just been cancelled but that we could make the early flight if we hurried."

Molly speaks next. "So we checked our

308

stuff real fast, then rushed — I mean, ran like track stars, even Mr. Dimming — down to the gate to get that early flight."

"Nobody thought about me?" I ask.

Silence again.

Finally, Elena says, "I did. I was the first one to board the plane. Just as I gave my boarding pass to the agent, I reminded Mr. Dimming that you were missing."

Mr. Dimming again twists from one foot to the other. "I was so busy — trying to count heads and check seat assignments and deal with everybody's carry-on bags — so I asked the kids to call you at home. I knew Rose, at least, had your number in her cell phone."

All eyes shift to Rose. She looks at the floor, then slowly, she looks at me. A tear runs down her cheek. "You couldn't have made it there in time anyway. I . . . I picked up my phone to call you. I flipped it open, then I looked at the rest of the kids on the team." She pauses.

I could imagine them standing there, thinking about the chance to be on *Good Morning America,* with that huge trophy . . . and me.

Rose continues in a whisper. "We looked at each other. Everyone made just a tiny head shake — no."

All of them? I shiver.

Rose sniffles and whispers finally, "So I closed the phone and we got on the plane. I . . . I never made the call."

How can silence be so loud?

Mr. Dimming finally says quietly, "I'm so very sorry, Melody. So sorry."

Rose bursts into tears then and puts her head down on her desk.

"Just before the competition," Molly explains, "a reporter from the *Washington Post* came to interview the team. But he left when he found out you weren't there."

Connor walks up to the front of the room then, picks up the ninth-place trophy, and brings it to me. He stammers and licks his lips. "Uh, the team kinda wants you to have this, Melody. Sorta to make up." He places it on my tray.

The thing is small, made of cheap plastic that has been painted to look like metal. The name of the school is even spelled wrong on the faceplate.

I look at the ugly little statue, and I start to giggle. Then I crack up. Finally, I roll with laughter. My hand jerks out and hits the trophy — I'm not sure if it was an accident or not — and it falls to the floor, breaking into several pieces.

The class stares at me in surprise. When

310

they see that I'm not going to go ballistic on them, they finally start to laugh as well — a little. Even Rose sniffs and smiles.

"I don't want it!" I finally type. Then, turning the volume as loud as it will go, I add, **"You deserve it!"**

Still laughing, I click on the power to my chair, do a smooth turn, and roll myself out of the classroom.

CHAPTER 33

Fifth grade is probably pretty rocky for lots of kids. Homework. Never being quite sure if you're cool enough. Clothes. Parents. Wanting to play with toys and wanting to be grown up all at the same time. Underarm odor.

I guess I have all that, plus about a million different layers of other stuff to deal with. Making people understand what I want. Worrying about what I look like. Fitting in. Will a boy ever like me? Maybe I'm not so different from everyone else after all.

It's like somebody gave me a puzzle, but I don't have the box with the picture on it. So I don't know what the final thing is supposed to look like. I'm not even sure if I have all the pieces. That's probably not a good comparison, since I couldn't put a puzzle together if I wanted to. Even though I usually know the answers to most of the questions at school, lots of stuff still puzzles me.

Penny came home from the hospital with bumps and bruises, a cast, and a new red hat. Doodle is back in her arms. They're spoiling her rotten. That's okay with me. Even Butterscotch is treating Penny like she's an injured puppy. The dog has brought all her favorite stuffed toys into Penny's room, like gifts.

Today I'm working on Miss Gordon's autobiography project. Mrs. V has Elvira plugged into the computer. Classical music is softly seeping from her new iPod. I hear soft purple.

This is going to take a while. So much is stuffed inside my mind. I have lots to say and just one thumb to say it with.

I guess I'll start at the very beginning. . . .

Words.
I'm surrounded by thousands of words. Maybe millions.
Cathedral. Mayonnaise. Pomegranate.
Mississippi. Neapolitan. Hippopotamus.
Silky. Terrifying. Iridescent.
Tickle. Sneeze. Wish. Worry.
Words have always swirled around me like snowflakes — each one delicate and different, each one melting untouched in my hands.

Deep within me, words pile up in huge drifts. Mountains of phrases and sentences and connected ideas. Clever expressions. Jokes. Love songs.

From the time I was really little — maybe just a few months old — words were like sweet, liquid gifts, and I drank them like lemonade. I could almost taste them. They made my jumbled thoughts and feelings have substance. My parents have always blanketed me with conversation. They chattered and babbled. They verbalized and vocalized. My father sang to me. My mother whispered her strength into my ear.

Every word my parents spoke to me or about me I absorbed and kept and remembered. All of them.

I have no idea how I untangled the complicated process of words and thought, but it happened quickly and naturally. By the time I was two, all my memories had words, and all my words had meanings.

But only in my head.

I have never spoken one single word. I am almost eleven years old. . . .

ABOUT THE AUTHOR

Sharon M. Draper is a *New York Times* bestselling author and recipient of the Margaret A. Edwards Award honoring her significant and lasting contribution to writing for teens. She has received the Coretta Scott King Award for both *Copper Sun* and *Forged by Fire* and was most recently awarded the Charlotte Huck Award for *Stella by Starlight*. Her *Out of My Mind* has won multiple awards and was a *New York Times* bestseller for over three years. She lives in Cincinnati, Ohio, where she taught high school English for twenty-five years and was named National Teacher of the Year. Visit her at SharonDraper.com.

The employees of Thorndike Press hope you have enjoyed this Large Print book. All our Thorndike, Wheeler, and Kennebec Large Print titles are designed for easy reading, and all our books are made to last. Other Thorndike Press Large Print books are available at your library, through selected bookstores, or directly from us.

For information about titles, please call:
(800) 223-1244

or visit our website at:
gale.com/thorndike

To share your comments, please write:
Publisher
Thorndike Press
10 Water St., Suite 310
Waterville, ME 04901